What The]

A guide to finding the career you never knew you wanted

By
Alexander Lucksmith
Pigeonpine Press
Copyright 2021

Introduction

Auto-body apprentice - infomercial actor - caretaker for the disabled - acupuncture trainee - herbal pharmacist- tea salesperson -retail manager - massage therapist- social media manager - political canvasser - video game tester - and some kind of teacher...

I started with the jobs I thought I **should** do. But *should* is a loaded term. Did I feel like I *should* because of other people's expectations? Or I *should* because that is what I went to school for? The more I worked for what I *should* be doing, the more I realized I *should* be doing something else. What about working in what I was good at? Just because I had a talent for something didn't make me feel much better about going to work each day. Maybe I just needed to make money? Grind through work and live for the weekend? But at 40-60 hours a week, I was feeling so ground-up that all I wanted to do was sleep through my days off.

Then one day a person offered me an empty room, a pile of laptops, and the mission "do whatever you want, just get more kids to finish school". And for the first time I was doing what I wanted to be doing. It wasn't because I *should* be helping others, or because I was good at it, and the pay was nothing to write home about, but it challenged me in a way that no other job did. It was, and still is, the hardest job I've ever had, and I wouldn't have traded it for anything.

My original batch of students are just about grown up. They are getting their first jobs, looking into colleges, and thinking about what their lives might look like in the not-so-distant future. So I wrote them this book to hopefully save them a bit of pain and frustration.

To my "Punks":

Sometimes we just have to work to survive. But I hope you will remember to keep asking yourselves what it is you *want*. And that might change, or show up in unexpected ways. If it wasn't for a lifetime of wrong turns in my career, I wouldn't have ended up at the doorstop of our classroom. I never imagined I would be your teacher for all these years, and you all have brought me more joy and fulfillment than anything else I've accomplished. I'm never more than a shoe-throw away if you ever need me to get you back on track. This book is for you; I hope you cringe at every dad-joke and remember all the good times we had.

Notes on the 1st edition:

"Have no fear of perfection, you'll never reach it"
-Salvador Dali

My editor wears a wedding ring I gave her and my consultant is a golden mutt named "TokiDoki", I could not ask for a better team. You will find mistakes; enjoy them. If you get stuck in your search and need help, if you want to argue, if you would like your job or interview to be in the next edition, drop me a line.

Building your Resume

A resume is a conversation piece, not a confessional. It should inspire a conversation about the position and highlight the unique things that make you perfect for this job.

Most of you reading this probably don't have a lot of job experience under your belt. That is ok; we just need to reposition some of the other experiences you've had. School, clubs, church, volunteering, and even hobbies are all good sources for showing off your skills. Just because it seems easy or natural to you doesn't mean a potential employer wouldn't be impressed by it. If you got an attendance award at school for not missing any classes in a semester, that's something to feature. It might seem like it took no effort on your part, but companies want to know you are reliable and dependable and one of the best ways to show that is through your attendance.

To break it down even more, imagine you participated in high school theater. Dancing means you have endurance on your feet. Singing shows dedication and willingness to practice a skill. Acting requires putting yourself in uncomfortable situations in front of strangers and colleagues. If you worked behind the scenes there are a lot of skills you may have that don't apply to the job you are looking for, but it shows your willingness and ability to learn a new skill. For example, learning how to run a light and sound board is way more complicated than learning how to use a cash register, and a good manager will see that. It might not seem like someone would value those efforts, but anyone can put in a good effort if they are getting paid to do so. Someone who can show dedication without compensation, in clubs, sports, and hobbies, is demonstrating their true potential.

A good way to find your "hidden skills" is to imagine you are hiring for the position you are applying for. Let's say you run a lot of bake sales for your club. If someone was going to take over for you, what would they need to do? Would they need to coordinate with everyone bringing baked goods? Would they need to talk to the school and set up posters? Would they need to manage the cash box and report the earnings? Right there are three skills that 90% of companies are looking for: Collaborating with others, project management, and cash handling. As I am writing this, there are over 400,000 jobs available on LinkedIn where project management is a desired or required skill. And every retail and food service opportunity out there is going to require coordinating with other people and dealing with money. What seems like a simple bake sale can easily become the cornerstone of your whole application.

Tips for your resume

- Your name should be at the top in big bold letters. When an employer is looking through 50 resumes to find the one they were interested in, they don't want to have to hunt to find it. Same with contact info, keep it easily visible and near the top

- Make an effort to pair an example with every skill or trait you are claiming. Don't just say "attention to detail", instead try "My attention to detail led me to being selected as our school newspaper editor. Even when it seems obvious like "top salesperson", elaborate a bit. Top out of how many people? For how long?

RESUME

- Make your resume unique, but not obnoxious. Little things make a big difference, like a printed border or nice paper. No need for crazy fonts or graphics unless that is part of your pitch. Even then it's a gamble.

- The general order, or "hierarchy" for your resume should be name, contact info, job experience, education, volunteering and awards. Unless your education is the key to your resume, it is generally less important than other experiences you've had.

- Each job should have the company name, your position, and the dates you worked there. If you are still at that job, put -present after your hire date. Some people will break down their jobs individually at the same company. Like if they went from barista to assistant manager they would list that as two positions with two separate dates. I don't like this because it weakens your position. If you were a barista for two years and a manager for three months that is nothing you need to "confess" in your resume. But if they ask at the interview, be honest. There are some exceptions to this, like if the two positions were in completely different departments, but in general each company should only get one spot on your resume.

- Each job should list 3-4 skills or duties of that position. Try for a bit more than "worked the cash register". Instead add a bit more: "handled cash, card, EBT transactions, refunds, and exchanges". It's the same as "working the register", but shows you can do more complicated tasks than just swiping a piece of plastic.

- Most recruiters are huge sticklers for spelling and grammar. I'm not, and I don't think they should be either. Sure if you misspell "attention to detail" it undermines your point, and there are managers who will discard a perfect candidate over a misspelled word or two.

- Keeping your resume to one page is helpful if you are printing and delivering them to companies. Stapled pages get lost and double-sided printing can often be missed. Again the idea here is to make it convenient for the humans who read stacks of these things. If your resume is online, go nuts with the length. Bots and humans alike will be fine with a digital resume that is more robust than the printed version.

- Lots of people will tell you to have a "mission statement" or summary at the top of your resume. I think this is useless. I've never read one of these that made me more curious about the person, and usually they sound like some baloney "execuspeak".
 The exception to this is if you are applying for something online. The bots that scan resumes for job postings look for certain keywords and this can be a great place to cram a bunch of them in. In that case, you can actually make your lack of experience work for you! For example, if the position asks for experience "working with seniors" but you have none. In your mission statement you could say "while most of my experience is with students, I'm looking forward to a career working with seniors". All the filtering bot will see is that your resume is a match for the phrase "working with seniors"!

- Speaking of bots, go ahead and put your resume on LinkedIn. I don't like shilling for one particular company, but they are the best game in town as of 2022. Not only can you generate a PDF of your resume whenever you want, you can also apply for most jobs online with a single click. Plus, as a manager I appreciate being able to look up your publicly posted info whenever I need to. It's so much more convenient than digging through a stack of printed papers or searching my inbox for an attachment.

- Cover letters - some positions ask for them, while others don't. When asked for, a good cover letter can be a game changer. This is your chance to showcase skills and interests that set you apart from other applicants. In general, two paragraphs and a handful of bullet points are plenty.

In the first paragraph, mention what it is about this company that made you apply. It could be that they make the best Unicorn Latte in the country, or that their commitment to renewable resources is why you always shop there. Whatever it is, find a reason that is unique to them.

The second paragraph should illustrate why you are either more qualified than the position demands, or have a special exemption to the posted requirements. For example, if you wanted to work at a museum because you grew up hunting fossils with your grandfather, who happens to be a paleontologist, this is something you could mention in your letter. It shows personal interest and a connection to the work the museum is doing. If you meet all the job requirements, this might put you above someone with similar qualifications. If you don't quite have the qualifications they are looking for, this can save your application from going directly in the trash.

RESUME

The third paragraph (or bullet points) is a chance to highlight any special skills or connections to the company you may have that weren't on the application. You might not feel confident putting a bake-off award on your resume, but if you are applying for your first bakery job, the cover letter would be a great place to showcase it.

- Lastly, call the store after you've applied and ask to speak to a manager (but try not to call during their busiest times). Let them know you applied and would be happy to answer any questions they have after they've had a chance to take a look at your application. This way, when they look through that stack of papers, they have a voice and personality to go with the name. You can do this in person too, but bring an extra resume to leave with them.

ACEING THE INTERVIEW

The best interviews I've had were the ones where it felt like I was talking to a stranger at a dinner party. Finding common ground is a great way to keep the rhythm of the interview natural, and is easier than most people think. With a few tips, you can turn a conversation with a stranger into your new career.

I used to have these tricks for conducting interviews. When someone would come into the tea shop, I wouldn't greet them right away. I'd see what they did when they came in. Shy folks would usually mill around the store, not saying anything until someone approached them. Not ideal in a job where it would be their responsibility to go up to people, like in sales. On the other hand, some people would go straight to the counter and say "I have an interview". No introduction, no greeting, not even a "how are you doing?". Sure, it was more direct, but this person is your future co-worker. Wouldn't you want to meet them? Maybe ask a few questions that you don't want to ask the boss? The best folks were the ones that would come in, introduce themselves, and make some small talk with the clerk.

- Ideal candidates dress in something sharp, clean, and have some kind of professional purse or messenger bag. You don't have to come in looking like a runway model, but anything that is within your control (like makeup, hair, and shoes) is something I'd look for. People who haven't recently shaved where they usually shave (like neckbeards or untrimmed sideburns), dirty clothing or clothes with holes in it, anything with lots of branding or graphics, or anything that is made more for sports than the office were red flags for me. Clean shoes

INTERVIEWING

are more important than fancy shoes, and a good fitting polo is better than a baggy button-up. Hair and makeup generally don't influence the decision as much as one would think. Better to feel confident than overdone.

- A splash of deodorant and a swish of mouthwash before you come in the door can make a big difference. It wasn't uncommon that someone would be a good candidate but would either have terrible B.O. or bad breath. It was such a bummer because no one wants to say "hey, we thought you were great, but smelled super funky". Same goes for spraying on Axe or dousing yourself in perfume. In your bag, keep some emergency supplies. Things like wet wipes, stain remover, hygiene products, and mints (or gum, but don't chew it during your interview).

- Keep extra copies of your resume in a protected case or folder. In a pinch, fold them in half and put them in a book. Better to have one sharp crease than a bunch of wrinkles.

- Leave your sunglasses and hats in your bag as well. Subconsciously it makes it look like you are hiding something, and no manager wants to go digging for the truth. If you can't wear it in a courtroom, don't wear it to your interview. The phone goes in your bag as well, and turn it off before you drop it in. Even silent mode fails when that alarm you forgot starts going off.

- Lastly, my secret weapon; a notebook and pen. Managers will typically tell you that they will be taking notes and not to worry. You can do the same thing. Not only does this show that you are prepared and engaged,

INTERVIEWING

it honestly helps as well. If the interviewer tells you something interesting you want to remember or you think of a question you want to ask, write it down and get it out of your head. Interestingly, the interviewer will sharpen up as well. People pay more attention to what they say when they know someone is taking notes. It can turn an everyday interview into something that sticks out in their memory a bit more.

- When it was time to start the interview I'd say "hey, let me make you something to drink, we'll start the interview in a few. How was your drive in?" Their answers here would tell me half of what I needed to know right then and there. I found that people I hired that accepted the tea could also accept help, training, and even criticism better than those who turned it down. Something about being comfortable in an uncomfortable situation was exemplified by taking the tea. They would score bonus points if they either knew what they wanted (showing they had knowledge of the store and it's products) or if they gave me some guidelines and let me choose. Even rejecting my suggestion showed they had standards and wouldn't get steamrolled by the company or it's customers, more on that later.

- Saying "anything's fine" was not a great answer. It might seem like this shows flexibility and "go with the flow", but it gives the manager nothing to work with. This might seem like too much importance on a cup of tea, but consider this. If I hired an "anything's fine" person, how would I know what motivates them? If I give them a task they can't do or don't want to do, how can I trust that they would speak up? And if they don't have any wants, what is going to motivate them to work hard in this position?

- Even if they are not thirsty, they should still take the tea. The manager is offering an olive branch, a symbol of goodwill. They didn't have to drink it, but they should have accepted it. This might seem contrary to the "stand up for what you want" I said a moment ago, but there is something in sales psychology we can take here. Accepting a favor creates a bond and trust between people. If I offer a sample to a customer and they take it, we have built trust. Instead of getting generic answers from them, I get to hear what they actually want and what is actually getting in the way of shopping with me today. That makes it a lot easier to accommodate and negotiate than a generic "no, thank you". If I'm trying to sell you on taking this job, I want to be able to accommodate and negotiate as well.

- "How was your drive in?" tells me how they structure their time and how they generally respond under stress. If someone said "Oh, it was great. There was some traffic, but I still got here early enough to get a pretzel" that is as close to a perfect response as I could ask for. They are not complaining to a stranger about how bad traffic was, they are not stressing over the delay, and they found something to do when they arrived early. So when I think about how this person would handle the register, it tells me that they can face challenges with a positive attitude and know what to do with themselves even when no one is giving them directions. On the other hand, someone who goes on and on about how the traffic was bad or how they couldn't find parking shows me that they don't handle stressful situations as well. It could be they didn't prepare or manage their time well, or it could be that they take issues out of their control as personal problems. So what happens when they have to come every day? Are they always going to be stressed, late, and angry? Not the kind of person I want in my store.

- So at this point I've seen how they dressed, when they've arrived, who they talked to when they got to the shop, and seen how they respond to a couple of casual questions. Between this and their resume, I've already made my decision. And frankly, I'm not alone. Most interviewing managers make up their mind in the first 5 minutes. The rest of the interview is to confirm or challenge their decision. If a person comes in late and with a bad attitude but interviews well, I know that they might do great at customer service, but are almost guaranteed to have issues with the company or their co-workers. No one can be in "customer service" mode 24/7 and true feelings are going to come out at some point, I learned that the hard way.

One time I was coming home from work on the bus. It was around 11:00 at night and I'm on the phone with another manager. Corporate was pushing us to sell more and more, but there are only so many people to try to convince in a day. I'm just blowing off steam, talking about how I hated being pushy especially with products I didn't believe in. Little did I know, 3 seats behind me was one of the biggest customers that day. The next morning, the most brutal review was posted with all the "insider knowledge" I was talking about on the phone. Sure, it was an embarrassing coincidence, but it was my own unhappiness that caused it. I didn't feel like I could talk to my manager about the issues, I made the company's bad decisions my own problem, and I couldn't leave work at work so I ended up taking all that stress home with me, via the bus. That's not to say we shouldn't complain about work or de-stress with others, but I wonder how many times before that day I had been on the same bus complaining on my phone. How many days did I take my unhappiness home with me, and then brought it back the next day? At a certain point, I'm sure my unhappiness became a self-fulfilling prophecy. I expected stressful and difficult days, so I ended up with stressful and difficult days.

If an interviewee is supposed to show me their best self, and they are already bringing me stress and complaints, there is nothing I can do to fix that. I hope the best for them, but their resume is already on the way to the trash can. If someone comes in early, is sociable, and seems generally engaged, it almost doesn't matter if they bomb the interview after that. A good manager can see through a bad moment to a good employee.

The interview should flow like a conversation. It's not a quiz and they aren't looking for a "gotcha". Remember, you are in that seat because they need you. You are the missing element they are looking for. So when they ask a question, take a moment and think about the answer. You can even say "good question, let me think about that for a second.". A good interviewer would rather have the honest answer than the first thing that pops into your head. In one of my first interviews, I was applying for a phone customer service position. When I was asked "what is your worst quality" I blurted "my patience". Not only was that the absolutely wrong answer for a job dealing with cranky people, it was also totally untrue! I interviewed with them a few years later and they still remembered that answer, but instead of it working against me we just laughed it off like a joke.

When the interviewer talks, be curious about what they are saying. They are human too, they want to feel like what they are saying matters and is interesting. Without getting too off track, ask them questions as well. If they mention they need to hire more people than usual, ask them why. Not only does this keep the conversation from being turned into a presentation, it also gives you more opportunities to show off. Let's say that the reason they are hiring more is because a new product is out that everyone is crazy for. Now you can show off your knowledge of the product or talk about how you used to handle crowds when you worked for your school's stadium as a ticket taker.

Whenever you can, and this is super important, tie a specific example with your answer. If the question is "what would you bring to the team" and you want to highlight your cash-handling skills, don't just say "I'm good at handling money and giving change". Instead try "I'm great at handling cash. For example, I was made our club treasurer and handled the cash boxes at our school carnivals and fundraisers". Anybody can make claims, but the true champs can back it up with facts. This is especially true for anything you didn't list on your resume or job requirements you have limited experience with. Like if the job involved restocking shelves, but you have never restocked before, you could talk about how you organized your closet by color, or how you always put away the groceries and clean the fridge. Just because you may have only used a skill for

INTERVIEWING

your own benefit or enjoyment doesn't make it any less valuable.

    I once hired a design intern because they listed their Tetris high score and Playstation achievements on their resume. For someone who had no other relevant experience, this really became the focus of our interview. Anyone who was devoted and focused enough to be a completionist in a game and then push themselves even higher was worth a hire. They used other examples from their day to day life to fill in the gaps in their resume as well. An attendance award became an example of showing up on time. An honors class in ceramics became a discussion of how they dealt with a difficult situation (while also highlighting their creative/artsy side). So even though more experienced designers were applying, no one else showed the same drive and discipline as this person. Years later, this same person is one of the youngest senior designers in their studio and just bought their first house. In the end, I can teach someone Photoshop, I can't teach them to be detail oriented or resilient.

    Confidence can seem like a bad word during an interview. Like you are bragging or making yourself overly important. That's not the case. Confidence is showing that while you appreciate this opportunity, the company needs to offer you more than just a paycheck in exchange for your time. They need to provide you with the tools and environment you want to be in. No need to brag or exaggerate, being genuine is much more important than being superior sounding.

INTERVIEWING

An important piece to confidence is showing your positive side. My old boss called it "keeping it positive and progressive". Meaning that confidence doesn't come from pushing other people down, it comes from drawing other people up. There is a common interview question that goes "tell me about a time you had a conflict with a co-worker and how did it resolve". If you start off by saying how bad this co-worker is and how badly they treated you or a customer or whatever, it shows you focused on the negatives instead of the solutions. You don't have to make them look like an angel, but there is a big difference between "this person was really mean to me" and "we got off on the wrong foot and never found a chance to resolve it". This goes for companies and customers as well. Even if your last job was with a garbage company (meaning a terrible company, not a company that deals with garbage) trash talking them is not going to score you any points. When you talk about others try to give credit and take responsibility, not the opposite.

These hacks go back to that "dinner party" vibe you want to cultivate during your interview. But don't skip one of the basic steps in exchange for an advanced technique. No amount of mirroring or eye contact is going to make up for strong B.O. and a stained shirt. Number one on the list is eye contact. This is the most basic way humans build trust. If you are looking down or your eyes are distracted or darting away the person talking to you is going to notice each time. The eyes tell the listener much more than we give them credit for. There is evidence that when someone is recalling a memory, they will look up. If they are making up a story, they tend to look to the left. So imagine what message it sends if the candidate's eyes are looking all over the place. If that much eye contact with a stranger is difficult for you, look at the space between their eyes. Dwight Schrute wasn't kidding when he offered that advice on The Office.

Mirroring is like the next level of eye contact. While you want to bring your own energy and personality to the party, copying the tone and feel of the manager can go a long way. You don't have to clone them or match their accent, but find the halfway point between their personality and yours. Notice what kind of language they use as well. Is it all industry terms and jargon, or is it casual and slang? Some managers only want to talk in formal terms. And that is ok, it keeps everyone on the same page and lessens the chance of misunderstanding. A quiet manager might get overwhelmed by someone coming in with a lot of volume and energy. A more intense interviewer might find someone being too quiet and calm as being "under-enthusiastic".

Never go more casual in your vocabulary than a Disney movie, even if the manager does. That means no swearing, drugs, drinking, or sexual references. I've heard from dispensary managers that when an interviewee only wants to talk about how much they like pot, they know they are most likely not a good fit. It's not because of the pot use (which would be ironic) but because the person is using interview time to highlight their habits and not their skills. It would be different if they were talking about cultivation or harvesting, but no boss in any industry wants to hear "yo, I got so blazed last night I forgot to set my alarm". So if the conversation

INTERVIEWING

is casual, keep it casual, but pretend your grandmother is listening from the next table over.

    Keep your hands where the other person can see them. The hands symbolize trust in our subconscious. If you are hiding your hands behind your back or stuffing them in your pockets, it's like you are saying "I have something to hide". Same goes with fidgety hands or touching your face often. Without looking like a mime, try to keep your hands visible and your palms open. Try not to cross your arms, bounce your legs, or point your toes in. A good practice is to look in a mirror before you go and jump up and down while cheering yourself on. I mean hands in the air hooting and hollering, saying things like "You got this!" and "This is going to go great"! Something about seeing ourselves be excited and confident, even in the privacy of our own home, gives us permission to be that way in the "real world".

    Toward the end of the interview, they are going to ask if you have any questions. This is like the finale to a big dance number. You want to ask questions that seem organic, relevant, and haven't been addressed yet. As tempting as it is, be careful looking for these questions online. Otherwise you'll find one good sounding question and will just be waiting to launch it as soon as you can. Trying to shoehorn in a memorized question instead of coming up with one on the spot rarely works. Managers have heard them all. Heck, they have probably used them in the past themselves! If you have a question you really love, or something you don't want to forget, write it down in your "secret weapon" notebook from earlier. That way you don't have to juggle it in your head with everything else going on.

INTERVIEWING

A good one to keep in your notebook is "why do you work here?". It's a very personal question and can tell you a lot about the company. If they say things like "good work life balance" or "great opportunity for promotion" these can be signs of a job that will take care of you. Rarely will anyone say "because the pay is amazing" so listen for things like "we make sure there is a clear track for advancement" or "there is a great benefits package". This is also where the red flags come in. A big one is "there is a good sense of teamwork and community". Sure, there can be, but that also can be code for "we expect you to do more work because otherwise you are letting others down". Places that treat their employees like cattle or indentured servants do a great job of pretending to care. If the interviewer seems depressed, exhausted, or frustrated, it usually means they have pressure wearing on them, and that pressure almost always comes down the pipe to the people below, namely you.

At the end, thank them for their time. When I am interviewing for a position I love to ask "do you have many more interviews today?" This gives me a chance to sympathize with them if they have a long day ahead or celebrate with them if they are almost done for the day. It also gives me an inside look at what I'm up against in terms of competition. If they offer me a position but the manager says "I don't have a lot of interviews today, there are just not a lot of people applying" it means I can put the screws to them a bit when negotiating salary. If there are dozens more interviews, it means I need to do something extra to stand out.

INTERVIEWING

A day or two later thanking them for their time and telling them you look forward to talking with them soon can help improve your chances of being hired significantly. A thank-you email or text is enough for most entry-level jobs. But if the competition is heavy, go for the hand-written card. Those cards, even if they are just glanced at, will sit on a desk all day. No one wants to throw away a pretty card, especially if it says something nice about them like "I really appreciate how you went out of your way to make me feel comfortable and made me a cup of tea. I would be honored to work for a company that promotes that kind of culture". Just like the interview and the resume, this highlights a quality (making people comfortable) and showing a specific example (making the cup of tea). It doesn't need to be long, but 3-4 sentences is the sweet spot for most notes. If you have a common interest (like a sports team you both like, a game you both play, ect...) this is the time to drop that reminder. A little "Go 49ers" before the "Sincerely" at the bottom of your letter will go a long way with the human inside the manager who is looking for someone to talk about the game with on Monday mornings.

I JUST GOT OFFERED A JOB!
Sweet! Time to make that cash!

Let's talk about the green elephant in the room. The most awkward part of the hiring process is often around money. Salaries are usually the biggest expense a company has, so whenever they can shave money off that bill, they will. The question will usually come up "how much are you looking for in this position" or "what salary range are you expecting". This is where your research beforehand will make a big difference. Before you accept an offer, see what people with a similar job title are making. If you have a special skill or experience, make sure to adjust for that as well. When they ask, be confident and concise. Don't waiver or back off. Present the number you have in mind and let it hang there. So for example, if you are applying for a fast food position and most of the places in the area are offering $15 an hour but the sign out front says $14 an hour, still tell them $15. The worst thing you can do is say "but that is negotiable". Well now you've basically said "I deserve this amount but I'm willing to work for less than I am worth".

Some companies make it sound like you would be lucky to work for them. This is an old-school way of interviewing that beats the candidate down, even if the manager wants to hire them. The idea is that by making the potential employee feel small, the company would have more leverage in negotiating a salary. If someone feels like they just barely qualify for the job, they are probably not going to rock the boat and ask for fair or adequate compensation. Same goes for companies that try to "corporate" the person to death. They will make it sound like everything is out of their control and compensation is non-negotiable. I've never changed my mind on hiring someone because they asked for more money after I offered them the position. I might not have been able to give it to them, but the request never left me second guessing my decision to hire them. Be extra cautious if they ask about how much you made in your last job. In some states this is illegal, especially if they haven't offered you a number first.

Whatever they counter with, stick to your guns. A good response to their argument could be "I totally understand your position. But with my skills and experience I bring more to the table than other applicants. The industry average is $15 an hour so I would be looking for employment that met that expectation".

It might be hard to pass on a job over what seems like a small amount, but remember that you are setting yourself up for future success, especially if the company offers raises as a percentage increase. 10% of $15 an hour is more than 10% of $13.50 an hour. But let's say the company can't or won't budge on the pay and you still want to work for them. There are other benefits you can leverage in exchange. For example, most jobs have paid time off. If a manager can't increase your starting pay, they may be able to add extra paid time off to your time bank. Or if you need to take Thanksgiving week off even though it is the busiest time of the year, you can ask for that instead of more pay.

Another tactic I like to use is called "The Fast Track". It's what I do after I've been given a low salary offer and can't get them to budge. I say "I still want to work with your company, but I need to get to $X per hour in the next 6 months. What can we do about putting me on a track for advancement so I can have a position that pays closer to my requirements". What you are saying here is "I'll take your lowball offer, but only if you tell me exactly when and how I would get a promotion". This is great if you want to move up the ranks of a company, especially if you are coming in for an entry level position. Hiring managers like to know you are going to stick around and that if they suddenly need a keyholder or assistant manager, there is someone interested in training for that position and moving up.

With anything you are negotiating, Get. It. In. Writing. That doesn't make it a legal contract, but it gives you something to show if the company is slacking or if the person who hired you leaves. You want to be able to hold them accountable for the promises the company made. Even if the person is who was responsible for the agreements has left the company, they represented and made deals on behalf of the organization. The new boss can still ignore the agreement, but that gives you leverage to renegotiate. If they still don't budge, go back to the section in this book on making a resume because you'll be wanting a new job soon.

ON-THE-JOB
Understanding the Paperwork

Once you have settled on a salary, it's time to sign the papers and make it official. You'll need to bring your I.D. and proof of citizenship. Usually, this means a driver's license and social security card, though if you are under 18 and have a school I.D. that can generally be used in place of a driver's license. A birth certificate can be a substitute for a social security card as well. Best of all would be an unexpired passport. This counts as both your proof of identity and your proof of work eligibility. If you don't have any of these documents, ask your employer for a list of acceptable replacements. An up-to-date list usually comes with the forms you will be filling out.

Next is the tax paperwork which can look a bit intimidating. For most jobs, you will be getting an "I-4" which allows the employer to hold a bit of your paycheck to cover your taxes at the end of the year. You will need your social security number, so make sure you have it with you. The "Personal Allowances Worksheet" can look overwhelming, so let's break it down. The worksheet helps you find how many "allowances" you can claim. An allowance is a decrease in the amount of money taken out of your paycheck and set aside for taxes.

The I-4

1. Enter "1" for yourself if no one can claim you as a dependent

If someone else can claim that they pay most of your expenses, this makes you a "dependent". Generally, if you still live with your parents, you are still a dependent.

2. Enter "1" if you are single and have one job, married and have one job...

ON-THE-JOB

If you have more than one job between you and your spouse, the government will want to withhold more money because your total income will be higher. Most of the time you will put a "1" in this column unless you have a second job or your spouse has a job.

3. Enter "1" for your spouse, but you may choose to enter "0"

If you are married and provide most of the money, put a "1" here. Even though your spouse isn't a dependent, this shows that your income is being used by more than one person and should be taxed less.

4. Enter the number of Dependents you will claim...

99% of the time, this will be your children. There are special circumstances where someone is dependent on you entirely (like an ill relative you take care of, or a cousin who lives with you) and you can "claim" them as well, but only if no one else claims them on their taxes and they don't file their own taxes.

5. Enter "1" if you will file as Head of Household

This is a special circumstance where someone is living with a partner and a child, but they are not married. A person has to pay at least half of the living expenses and have a dependent they are claiming on their taxes.

6. Enter "1" if you have at least $1,900 of child or dependent care expenses...

These expenses include daycare, pre-school, or service that cares for your dependent while you are at work. School fees for a dependent usually don't count here.

7. Child Tax Credit...

If someone has a child and they predict that they will make less than the limits listed on the form, they can claim additional allowances here.

Add lines A through G and enter the total here... You made it! This number will go into box #5 in the form below. Your employer will use that number to determine how much is withheld each paycheck

Most of the time, you will not need to use boxes 6 and 7. The first allows your company to withhold extra tax money from your check. This is useful if you had a side business and wanted to make sure you had enough in tax savings to cover that income as well. The second box tells them to hold NOTHING from your pay, which can be an issue if you end up owing taxes at the end of the year.

If you make a mistake on this form it's not the end of the world. Let's say you don't claim all of your allowances. This means your paychecks will be smaller since more money will be saved from each one. But at the end of the year this could mean a bigger refund. A refund is the difference between what was withheld for taxes and what you owe the government. On the other hand, if you claim too many allowances your paychecks will be bigger, but you may owe money when taxes are due. I'm not an accountant and this isn't tax advice, but in general it's better to withhold more and be surprised by a refund at the end of the year than the opposite!

ON-THE-JOB

You will also need to fill out your "direct deposit" information. This is how the company can put your paycheck directly in the bank as opposed to writing you a check each month. In general, it is best to do direct deposit. The money gets to you faster, there is no chance of you losing your check, and you still will get a "paystub" showing how many hours you worked and what you were paid. Most companies ask for a "voided check". This is literally a paper check with the word VOID written across it. They use the numbers at the bottom of the check to make a link with your bank. If you don't have checks, your bank can usually print you out a few for a small fee. Alternatively, they may ask for your "routing and account number". These can usually be found on your online banking profile, though it can take some digging.

If you decide not to use direct deposit, the company may offer a prepaid debit card. I've heard horror stories about these and they should be avoided as much as possible. Not only is your money harder to access, there are also fees for everything. Want to check your balance, get a replacement card, send money to someone else, or use your signature instead of your PIN number? There is a fee for each of those actions. If you don't have a bank account (which generally wouldn't charge any of those fees) ask for a paper check. It will take longer, but at least no one will charge you for looking at it! When you cash your paycheck, avoid "check cashing" places. They will have higher fees and have been known to try to lure people into payday loans (which is a whole downward spiral of bad news). Instead, most grocery stores will cash your check at the service counter for a small fee.

ON-THE-JOB

Lastly, a "non-compete" is usually signed when you start a job, but sometimes can happen at the end. It basically states that you can't reveal company secrets, steal their customers, or copy their business ideas. This document has a bit of a punch to it, so be careful. You can't go work at McDonald's then start your own burger place across the street and sell BigMarks and MarkFlurries. It sometimes states that you cannot work for a similar or competing businesses as well. Each state has different laws regarding this, so even if you agree to their terms, it does not mean the law will back them up. For example, if a barista in Oregon is making around $46,000 a year and has a non-compete stating they cannot work for another coffee shop for 4 years after termination, that contract is not enforceable. Oregon law sets the minimum salary at $104,000 for a non-compete to be legal and the longest length of time to be between 12-18 months. There are exceptions to this, especially if secret information or customer lists are part of the job, but it is always a good idea to know what an employer is trying to get away with as opposed to what they can actually get away with.

ON-THE-JOB
On The Job Woes

I wish I could tell you that every day at your new dream job will be perfect. It won't be, especially if you have to rock the boat with a request or a change. Here are a few tips to make your rough moments smoother.

I don't want to go to work today

Understandable. Some days you are just not feeling it. Maybe you are getting sick, feeling stressed, or have something fun come up. Whatever the reason, tell your manager as soon as you decide. Nothing ruins their day more than counting on who is coming in and then not having enough time to replace them.

Sometimes, a company policy will conflict with your needs for a day off, so if you have to say you are "sick". Managers know when you are faking, it's just not worth it to them to fight it. They may want to give you the time off as well, but are hamstrung by the same policies. But in general don't make a habit out of lying. Someone who mysteriously gets sick during finals week is not fooling anyone. If you need time off for homework, say so.

The flipside here is ditching because you are running late or have something more fun to do. I know, I just said sometimes we need a day off to go enjoy life. But to a certain extent we've made an agreement to suspend some good times in exchange for stability. If you can count on your job being there tomorrow, they should be able to count on you to show up. Worse than that is skipping because you overslept or just forgot. This isn't like school where the only person who sufferers is you. A whole team of people are expecting you to show up and a stressed out boss stresses out your co-workers too. Once every year it might be an acceptable mistake, once a month is ridiculous. This goes double for ditching on any shift you agreed to cover for someone else. These same policies go with running late as well. If you can, call and let someone know when you think you can make it. Try not to make it a habit of being tardy even if it seems like not a big deal. People might work hard to not make you feel bad, even if they are secretly annoyed or inconvenienced.

I want a promotion or raise

Every six months to a year is a reasonable time to ask for a raise. In that time, you should have improved your skills, increased your experience, and gained new responsibilities. The key here is not to blindside someone with this request. If in the middle of the day you say you want an extra dollar per hour, it's not going to happen. Instead, try this. Let your manager know you would like to talk with them about your future with the company. Reassure them that you are not quitting, but try to save the discussion for a set time and date.

Remember, you are in charge here. You are not begging for crumbs, you are making sure you get paid fairly for your work. Go in with the mentality that the company should be happy to pay you more instead of going through the cost and effort to replace you. This is not a battle, it is a team-building exercise.

When you sit down to chat, think of it like a second interview. Go through all the tips we've already talked about, but remember you already have the job! They already saw enough in you to hire you, now they need to keep you happy. A great line to start off is "I really enjoy working for this company and I want to keep advancing my career here. And to do so I need to be compensated for my increased experience and responsibilities". If you have any new job duties that weren't part of your original job description, now is the time to bring those up. Be careful not to sound like you are complaining, you want to get across that you appreciate the extra responsibility and trust. Highlight any accomplishments you've had since your last promotion. For example: your speed at the register, any special promotions you sold the most of, or any ideas that the company has used to make the workplace better.

When they ask what you want in terms of an increase, aim for a bit higher than what you actually want. If you want $1 more an hour, ask for $1.50 or $2. At worst, you will have to compromise down to what you really want, but at best they might agree with the better figure. If they say no, hit them with the line from the interview section: "What can we do about putting me on a track for advancement so I can have a position that pays closer to what I am looking for". Set a timeline and get it in writing "for your reference". If they won't budge and they won't make a plan with you, that is a pretty big red flag. You might want to polish up that resume and start searching.

I want to quit

Yeesh, this is the big one and it might seem like a painful or awkward step in your career. Everyone quits, and chances are your boss has left a job as well at some point. In fact, most of the people reading this book will have at least thirteen jobs in their lifetime, and hopefully that means you won't be fired twelve times.

Don't go out with a bang. You might have some fantasy of telling off your boss and tossing the store keys on the roof. It's a good dream, but it will bite you when you wake up. Most jobs will ask for references and a scorned supervisor is not a name you want to put on that list. Even worse is "employment verification". This is where an HR department will call your former job to make sure you worked during the timespan you listed on your resume. In theory, your job performance can't be talked about, but there is one sneaky question they can ask. "Is the employee eligible for rehire?" This is code for "did the employee do something so messed up that they can't come back". If you gave no notice, pissed off a bunch of people, or did something that hurt the company, those things might disqualify you from being rehired. Of course this is a huge red flag for anyone considering hiring you. A good exit from even a crappy company can make it easier to get into a job you love.

The best thing you can do is put it in writing. Make it short, sweet, and to the point. Wait until the end of the day and let your supervisor know you are "putting in your notice" and hand them the letter. Thank them for working with you (even if they seemed evil) and leave it at that. For most jobs, 2 weeks is plenty of notice. They should be able to find someone in that amount of time, and if they don't it's not your responsibility.

This is where some places will try to pressure you

to stay. They'll say things like "now is not a good time" or "you will be letting your team down". What they are really saying is "hiring and training for your position is a huge pain and I don't want to do it". Tough. They might also try to negotiate with you as well. The ball is in your court at this point and you might get that promotion or raise you were looking for. If they do offer you something, get it in writing and make them commit to a specific timeline. If they say "when something becomes available" or "we'll get you that raise soon" it's as good as nothing.

If the situation is unbearable, just dip. Hopefully things won't get to that point for you, but if they do you don't need to commit to any extra time. Still, give them a letter of resignation and make sure anything that is their property gets back to them.

I just got fired

Sorry bud. Even if you were expecting it, it doesn't feel good. Let's do some damage control.

Do you think this firing was fair? Did you no-call no-show or do something that you agree you should be fired for? It's a hard thing to admit, but sometimes we've messed up and we have to pay the price. That doesn't mean all is lost. You don't necessarily have to apologize, but try to thank your co-workers and managers for their time. Get anything back to them that they need (keys, uniforms, ect...) and try to get a receipt for their return. Chances are you have unpaid hours and in many states those have to be paid out within 48 hours. Just because you were let go doesn't mean everyone hates you, or that everyone agrees that you should be gone. And you never know when an old connection is going to have a good opportunity for you in the future, so try not to burn any bridges that you don't have to burn.

But what if you were fired unfairly? It happens all the time, especially in states that have "at-will" employment laws where they don't even need a reason to let you go. Honestly, the easiest thing to do here is move on. Follow the advice above and try not to let it drain too much out of you. If you can, get a signed termination slip with the reason listed. If you decide to file for unemployment, this is an important document to have. Any time cards or write-ups should go with you as well.

There are exceptions to the "let it go" mindset, and they get pretty rough. If you were the victim of harassment, racism, or sexism you need to report this in writing to the highest level you can reach in your company. If you work for a big retail or food service establishment, remember that you can report things to the corporate offices outside of your store. The next step is to file a report with your state's labor department and the federal Equal Employment Opportunity Commission. It can be intimidating, but you are not only helping yourself, but anyone else who may have been a victim as well.

Sometimes, the company will tell you that you must sign some forms before they send you your final paycheck. Even if this is "company policy" it does not trump "federal law". Be especially careful if you

ON-THE-JOB

see the words "arbitration" or "liability release". This can be a way that the company distances itself from any wrongdoing it may have done. Arbitration means that instead of going to court they can hire a service to negotiate for them. They typically find in favor of the company that hired them, and even if they find that you were punished unfairly, the penalties are not usually enforced. A liability release is similar, except neither side admits guilt or fault and agrees that no one will sue. Sometimes, even if you have signed these agreements, they are not enforceable. If you make under a certain amount or the company fired you for whistle-blowing, there are special rules that override other agreements.

If you need legal help from a lawyer but can't afford it, there may be options. If you are in college, check with your counselor there. Most schools have free legal help available to their students. Most states have a non-profit to help represent lower-income folks. It never hurts to drop them a line and see if they can help. Some lawyers will work on a "contingency" basis. That means they don't take any money from you, but they'll take their pay out of any settlement they reach with your former company. It can seem unpleasant and difficult, but remember you may be protecting or advocating for people who can't speak up.

COMMON RED FLAGS

Not all red flags mean you should go running away from a job. What is important is if you see a pattern. If every day you are fighting these issues, it might be time to move on. On the other hand, maybe your boss just needs a Snickers and a nap.

"We need you to come in on your day off/stay late/ come in early"

This is a request, not a requirement. Often managers will pressure you or flat-out tell you that you "must" come in. You don't, in about 90% of circumstances. If you are "required" then there are all sorts of laws to cover you. For example, if you get to work but you can't start working because the grill is down or a supply delivery hasn't come in, you still should get paid for the time you are there. If you are "on-call" there should be an agreement in place to compensate you for your time.

Another common tactic is that bosses will tell their employees to come in 10-15 minutes early to "get ready" for the day. Sure, if you are coming in to get a cup of coffee and watch TikToks, that is reasonable. Making yourself comfortable for the day isn't covered. But anything work related, including checking emails and doing things like scheduling, are to be done during paid time. Same with any kind of after-hours phone meeting, message checking, ect... In short, if you are doing something for work outside of scheduled hours, it's with your approval and you are on the clock.

RED-FLAGS

"We don't pay overtime"

Yes you do. There are federal and state laws that protect people from working more than a certain number of hours per day or per week. If they "make" you work overtime, those extra hours are paid at 1.5 times your hourly salary.

For example, if you work for 40 hours one week and they need you to come in for another 8 hour shift, they have to pay you "time and a half" for those 8 hours. Or, if you had to work 2 shift back to back in most states after 8-10 hours you get paid 1.5 times your rate. Each state has different laws on top of the ones for the whole country (those are called "Federal laws"). It's worth looking up the specific rules for your city and state to make sure you are not leaving money on the table.

"No one else on the team has a problem doing ..."

Sure, no one else wants to jeopardize their salary, career, and rent payments. Just because no one has the ability or motivation to speak up does not mean everybody is in agreement. And maybe you're caught in this position as well. Maybe if you know it's not right and you can't afford to speak up. On one hand we owe it to each other to speak up when injustice happens. On the other hand, we may have people dependent on us to keep working and bringing in a salary.

In instances like this, the best thing you can do is collaborate and document. The crap is going to hit the fan someday, and you better have an umbrella ready. Always save a copy of the hours you have worked somewhere besides a work computer. This can be as easy as taking a picture of your time card before you submit it. When your paycheck arrives, make sure that the total before taxes matches your expected compensation. If something doesn't match up, you'll have a paper trail to back up your claim. This also goes for any promises or disciplinary actions. Get it all in writing and then save a copy of it somewhere off site. I'll give two examples of why this is so important.

A few years ago I was consulting for a startup. Eventually I was set to revamp their payroll system. This meant going into their record system and transferring over the old records. I noticed that there had been a "correction" to everyone's time card before it was submitted for payment. It turned out the owner was "penalizing" employees for mistakes by taking away their worked hours. Because it was just 10-30 minutes each time, no one really noticed. For most of the staff this was their first job, so the variations between the hours they were working and the total they were getting paid seemed normal. This, or course, is illegal. If a person works those hour, they get paid those hours. An employer cannot penalize you for mistakes or accidents, even if it costs them money. It took me 2 full work days to gather the records for all of the current and past employees and in the end there was more than 200 hours of "penalized" time missing. But I wouldn't have been able to prove any of it without the records that each employee had kept. In the end, more than $2,800 in missing compensation was returned to the staff.

The second comes from Reddit. An employee started bringing in their own coffee pods to work to

RED-FLAGS

use in the office's coffee machine. They were able to buy their own pods for $.25 each instead of the office's price of $.50 for the ones they provided. Someone in a position above them got wind of this and threatened the employee with "theft of water" for using the machine without paying for a pod. They even went so far as to threaten to fire the employee if they kept bringing in the pods. The coffee loving employee knew this was bull, but without proof it would turn into the employee's word versus the manager's, which unfortunately usually favors the manager. So the employee asked for the coffee policy and the threat of termination in writing. They also took screenshots of the office chat system where the supervisor was making these claims. Once they had it all on paper, they went to the head of the department and asked if bringing in coffee was actually against the rules. Of course it wasn't, but no one had gone so far as to document what the supervisor had said. It turns out this same supervisor had made similar claims and threats to other people, but always denied it. Now, with actual proof, the company was able to do something about this power tripping manager.

"Employees are not allowed to discuss salary"

This is not only scummy thing to say, it's also illegal. Employees should share what they are getting paid because it strengthens their arguments for promotions and raises. It also helps root out racism and sexism where someone may be getting paid more or less depending on how the world identifies them.

RED-FLAGS
"You have to pay us for..."

No, just no. Nothing in a job should cost you. If a job has you "invest" in the product or purchase a "starter set" that's not a job. Unfortunately, a lot of these "jobs" are MLMs (multi-level marketing) where you are supposed to sell a product or service to people you know. The big catch here is that the real money comes from recruiting other people to sell for you. Because of this, recruiters will try to entice you with things like "unlimited income potential" or "being your own boss". They talk a good game, and that's how they make their money, not selling whatever product they are pushing you to sell.

Training as well. Any training you need specific to the company should be paid by the company and you should be paid for your time. A student of mine received a letter from a former employer billing them for their on-the-job training. Their argument was that the company had invested in the employee, and that when the employee quit they had not held up their end of the bargain. Of course, this was false. But plenty of people get caught in the trap where a disgruntled employer tries to get revenge by shorting their pay or holding final paychecks hostage.

Another one is "unlimited potential for commission". Some sales jobs will lean heavily on this, going so far as to pay you below minimum wage but bringing it back to legal levels with commission. So if your state has a $15 per hour minimum, a company can pay you $5 and then commission on top of that. If you have a rough day, the company has to make up the difference between your base pay and minimum wage.

RED-FLAGS

But it also means you start each day "in the hole" and have to earn your way out of it. Sometimes this can work to your advantage, but any job that has to gamble your salary against sales is going to have more tricks up its sleeve to keep you from your money. Unless you are strong in sales and don't mind taking a gamble, treat this job with caution.

How to use this book

Treat this book like an ice-cream shop. There are a lot of flavors here, and if you try to analyze them all, you are going to have a hard time making a choice. Pick a job category that interests you and leaf through it. You'll be surprised what options are available that you may have never considered before!

This is the "big question". Look through a section and see what statement jumps out at you. Sometimes the same question will appear in different sections, especially when it's in regards to salary or education.

Jobs with an extra title listed here are the entry level positions that can lead to the more advanced job. This is especially important if the career requires a lot of education since it can help you "test the waters" before you commit to college or training in that field.

This is expected job growth for 2021. Jobs with negative growth are at the end of the category in the "graveyard"

This is the average salary for this position in Oregon. The number come for a government institution and takes into account everyone reporting with that job title. So starting wages could be lower than this number, but the top salary could be much higher.

A short description and a joke. Remember, this should be fun! It isn't homework and the clock isn't ticking. The more relaxed you are, the more you are able to allow yourself to really picture yourself in the position you are meant to be in today.

HEALTHCARE

I want to help people move better

Occupational Therapists
Occupational Therapy Assistants | 14.10% | Master's degree | $ 94,420
If something happens and you can no longer button your shirt or play video games, this is the type of physical therapist that will get your shirt and game on.

Physical Therapists
Physical Therapist Assistants | 17.20% | Doctoral or professional degree | $ 92,026
When your legs don't work like they used to before. Not just a catchy song, but also what happens before you call a physical therapist.

Exercise Physiologists
| 8.40% | Bachelor's degree | $ 58,875
An athlete's best friend. You help set up their training programs and pass directions on to their personal trainers.

Athletic Trainers
| 19.40% | Bachelor's degree | $ 56,266
Arnold Schwarzenegger was one of these, and then he became the Terminator, and then the governor. A perfectly logical career path.

Healthcare

When people think of high paying jobs, "doctor" has to be near the top of the list. But "doctor" is a pretty broad term. Generally, we are talking about someone who heals other people and has been in school for a long, long time. But surprisingly there are tons of jobs in healthcare that pay well and don't require the time and expense of getting a doctorate. Sure, you might not be able to put "Dr." in front of your name, but being able to help people while earning enough for a house and a car is a pretty sweet gig.

Patience, listening, and attention to detail are all key skills here. Memorization and organization are pretty much required for any medical classes or degrees. The downsides of working in healthcare can be intense as well. You have pressure to take care of your patients on one side, and a heavy administrative burden on the other. Burnout is common, and turnover can be intense. Some careers in medicine can be hard to adapt to. If you have any phobias of bodily fluids, choose your career wisely. People will tell you that you get used to it, and you do, but there is a pretty big initial shock value to overcome. But it doesn't take a book to tell you what you get from this type of job. More than any other career path here, medicine makes the most direct impact on people. You get to improve, extend, and save the lives of others, and be paid well to do so.

HEALTHCARE

I want to make the most money

Obstetricians and Gynecologists

| 8.60% | Doctoral or professional degree | $255,601

Great career if you are interested in working with families. Like a plumber, except your dishwasher probably doesn't give birth to babies.

Family and General Practitioners

| 13.40% | Doctoral or professional degree | $205,880

This is your typical everyday doctor, usually has a good supply of lollipops and tongue depressors.

Dentists, General

| 10.10% | Doctoral or professional degree | $ 201,598

Four out of five dentists agree, A career that pays a quarter million dollars a year to help people with their teeth is a pretty good deal.

Nurse Anesthetists

| 25.60% | Master's degree | $184,300

You know those videos of people waking up from dental surgery and saying funny things? this person gets to see that everyday. They help sedate patients before major procedures and operations.

HEALTHCARE

I don't want to be in school forever

Cardiovascular Technologists
| 9.20% | Associate's degree | $ 87,127
Helps with heart surgery and cardio treatments. You are like a mechanic for a big fancy blood pump.

Radiologic Technologists
| 10.40% | Associate's degree | $ 77,818
Did you ever walk through one of those scanners at the airport and wish you could turn it into a full-time career in medicine? These folks run all of the amazing machines that look inside you.

Healthcare Social Workers
| 13.10% | Bachelor's degree | $ 76,930
This career helps people who need medical attention, support or services. They work between health care providers, facilities, and insurance companies to provide the best care to patients.

Respiratory Therapists
| 23% | Associate's degree | $ 73,655
Breathe in, breathe out. Okay, now help other people do the same thing and you've got a job.

HEALTHCARE

I don't want to deal with any patients

Medical and Health Services Managers

| 17.40% | Bachelor's degree | $ 117,197

If you love hospital cafeteria food but don't want to be a medical practitioner, this is the job for you. You manage the equipment, people, and resources of a hospital or Health Care Facility.

Environmental Science and Protection Tech

| 10.80% | Associate's degree | $ 59,576

In the old days you would just send somebody to drink out of a lake to see if it was poisonous. Instead, we have this job that uses laboratories and tests samples in the field.

Medical Records and Health Info Tech

| 11.10% | Postsecondary training (non-degree) | $ 51,622

You help keep track of patient records and progress. Kind of like all those stats on the back of a baseball card, but with markers for kidney function and blood pressure instead of home runs.

Biological Technicians

| 7.60% | Associate's degree | $ 43,459

You don't generally have to deal with patients, but you get to spend a lot of time looking through microscopes at tissue samples.

HEALTHCARE

I don't want human patients

Veterinarians

| 22.50% | Doctoral or professional degree | $ 108,175

They might come in scared, but if they get enough cheese and treats they'll be okay. I meant the pets, but I guess this works for the owners as well.

Zoologists and Wildlife Biologists

| 6.50% | Bachelor's degree | $ 75,712

If you ever thought about jumping over the rails at the zoo to get a closer look, this is the job for you.

Microbiologists

| 5.60% | Bachelor's degree | $ 65,558

Like a biologist, but smaller.

Veterinary Technologists

| 22.40% | Associate's degree | $ 37,660

If you love to pet animals, this is a good choice. You get to help them keep their tails wagging by performing basic procedures and assisting the veterinarian.

HEALTHCARE

Katie G.
Veterinary Technician

What do you make now compared to the when you started?
Now $18 an hour, previously it was $15 an hour. After I finish school that should go up a lot.

Why did you decide to work in this field?
To help animals. There are hard days, you will have to watch animals pass. But there are also days where you get to help all these little things. Plus, you get to see lots of weird stuff.

What career goal are you reaching for right now? How much work will it take and when will you get there?
Certification as a vet technician through a 2 year course. The rest is on the job training unless I decide to go to veterinary school.

If money wasn't an issue, would you change careers? If so, what would you do?
Maybe, I would go to school for teaching. All jobs are hard in their own way. It really matters that you feel that you have enough time with the people you love.

HEALTHCARE

I don't want to deal with blood

Pharmacists
Pharmacy Technician | 6.50% | Doctoral or professional degree | $ 144,764
A tough job. Most pharmacies are right across from the candy aisle, so you have to stare down that Snickers bar everyday. Besides that, pharmacists ensure the patient understands how to take their medicine, what side effects it may have, and what medications it may interfere with.

Podiatrists
| 1.70% | Doctoral or professional degree | $ 125,844
Do you want to work with everyone from athletes to grandparents? A podiatrist is a doctor that specializes in feet, like the famous Dr. Scholls. Relieving foot pain can greatly improve the quality of life for Don't worry, everybody washes up first.

Radiation Therapists
| 8.70% | Associate's degree | $ 106,950
They use radioactive things to treat disease. Like if a mad scientist wanted to use a giant ray gun to treat cancer instead of killing Batman. They even have a tool called a "nuclear scalpel", how cool is that!

Psychiatrists
Psychiatric Aides | 21.80% | Doctoral or professional degree | $ 102,650
Why can't you hear a psychiatrist using the bathroom? Because the 'p' is silent. I'm sure a psychiatrist would prescribe me something for all of these bad jokes.

HEALTHCARE

I don't want to deal with body fluids

Diagnostic Medical Sonographers

| 21% | Associate's degree | $ 94,871

They use wands that make whale sounds to make pictures of what's inside of you. I'm not exaggerating.

Genetic Counselors

| 0 | Master's degree | $ 93,052

You look at the genes of people to determine things like how future offspring might look. Pioneered by Dr. Lee and Dr. Levi when they were working on denim pants.

Audiologists

| 17.30% | Master's degree | $ 87,956

This is the doctor you go to see after you stand too close to the speakers at a concert. I said, THIS IS THE DOCTOR YOU GO SEE AFTER YOU STAND TOO CLOSE TO THE SPEAKERS AT A CONCERT.

Dietitians and Nutritionists

Dietetic Technician | 10.90% | Bachelor's degree | $ 73,465

A dietitian once told me that Lemonheads are not a fruit and that Hot Tamales don't count as ethnic food.

HEALTHCARE
I like to fix things

Biomedical Engineers
| 12.4% | Bachelor's degree | $ 87,571
These are the folks that will help us get our new robotic bodies in the future. Until then, they design technologies to help keep us healthy

Medical Equipment Repairers
| 9.40% | Postsecondary training (non-degree) | $ 76,033
"Well there's your problem, you filled your X-ray machine with Y-rays".

Orthotists and Prosthetists
Medical Appliance Technicians | 26.10% | Bachelor's | $ 71,322
Basically one step away from being Tony Stark. You help build and apply replacement limbs and accessories for people who need them.

Medical Equipment Preparers
| 10.30% | Postsecondary training (non-degree) | $ 43,200
The perfect job for germaphobes. You sterilize and clean all of the equipment in a hospital or healthcare facility.

HEALTHCARE

I want people to think I'm a wizard

Nuclear Medicine Technologists

| 9.50% | Associate's degree | $ 94,474

Assistant to the regional mad scientist. You help prepare and deliver radioactive medicine for people.

Magnetic Resonance Imaging Technologists

| 9.60% | Associate's degree | $ 94,135

You know the giant metal donut you see in every hospital show? These are the people that run it. MRI techs take millimeter thin images across a patient's body so doctors can make a diagnosis.

Speech-Language Pathologists

| 22.90% | Master's degree | $ 84,767

Helps people with speech impediments or language problems learn to overcome them. A really cool and overlooked career that changes lives just by helping people to talk.

Counselors

| 9.30% | Master's degree | $ 52,496

like a really good friend you have coffee with, except they don't judge you and they charge around $100 an hour.

HEALTHCARE
I want to help doctors

Dental Hygienists
Dental Assistant | 13.90% | Associate's degree | $ 89,356

Did you know Eminem did this for a while? He actually talks about it in one of his songs. "I'm a menace, a dentist, an oral hygienist". Though I don't think he was talking about assisting a dentist by cleaning teeth.

Surgical Technologists
| 11.30% | Postsecondary training (non-degree) | $ 60,489

You get to be in the surgery room but you don't actually have to stick your hands in anybody. Well, at least not that often.

Medical Assistants
| 24.30% | Postsecondary training (non-degree) | $ 42,869

A good gateway into medicine. You get to work with patients and doctors while helping them check patients in and take their vitals.

Phlebotomists
| 16.40% | Postsecondary training (non-degree) | $ 40,783

Like a medical vampire. You take blood from patients for tests, donations, and just for fun. Ok, maybe not just for fun.

HEALTHCARE

I want to be where the action is!

Surgeons
| 6.70% | Doctoral or professional degree | $ 284,501
Knife goes in, guts come out, everyone high fives.

Nurse Midwives
| 15.70% | Master's degree | $ 115,706
Were you really good at baseball and like to play with dolls? This is the job for you. You help directly with babies being born.

Licensed Practical and Licensed Vocational Nurses
Nursing Assistants | 10% | Postsecondary training (non-degree) | $ 59,046
These are the people you want to be the most nice to in a hospital. They manage most of your treatments, keep you safe, and help you get extra dessert.

Emergency Medical Tech / Paramedics
| 6% | Postsecondary training (non-degree) | $ 42,076
You get to drive the big truck with the lights on top of it that makes the wee-woo sound. Oh, you also get to save lives.

HEALTHCARE

I want to help people feel good

Clinical / Counseling / School Psychologists

| 18.50% | Master's degree | $ 91,902

The kind of doctor that uses talking to help make you feel like a better person. Sometimes you get to lay on a little couch just like in the movies.

Massage Therapists

| 26.20% | Postsecondary training (non-degree) | $ 63,376

People think massages are just for relaxing, but after a session their muscles work better, they have more energy, and are in less pain. Pretty cool.

Recreational Therapists

| 5.60% | Bachelor's degree | $ 58,766

Did you like making up games during recess? This career uses fun and games to help people build strength and recover from injury.

Rehabilitation Counselors

| 10.40% | Master's degree | $ 40,176

You hang out with cool folks who need a bit of help due to a disability or injury. Sometimes you go grocery shopping, sometimes you go to an amusement park.

HEALTHCARE

I want to help people move better

Occupational Therapists
Occupational Therapy Assistants | 14.10% | Master's degree | $ 94,420
If something happens and you can no longer button your shirt or play video games, this is the type of physical therapist that will get your shirt and game on.

Physical Therapists
Physical Therapist Assistants | 17.20% | Doctoral | degree $ 92,026
When your legs don't work like they used to before. Not just a catchy song, but also what happens before you call a physical therapist.

Exercise Physiologists
| 8.40% | Bachelor's degree | $ 58,875
An athlete's best friend. You help set up their training programs and pass directions on to their personal trainers.

Athletic Trainers
| 19.40% | Bachelor's degree | $ 56,266
Arnold Schwarzenegger was one of these, and then he became the Terminator, and then the governor. A perfectly logical career path.

HEALTHCARE

I want to help people see

Optometrists
| 6.40% | Doctoral or professional degree | $ 118,183
An eye doctor/wizard. You look into what is essentially a crystal ball, and from tiny clues can figure out what is going on with a person's vision.

Dispensing Optician
| 6.10% | High school diploma or equivalent | $ 43,712
You get to match lenses to frames and help people look stylish while also being able to see across the road

Ophthalmic Medical Technicians
| 16.30% | Postsecondary training (non-degree) | $ 43,471
When you get your cosplay contact lens stuck in your eye because you watched a YouTube video, these are the people that help fix it.

Ophthalmic Laboratory Technicians
| 18.10% | High school diploma or equivalent | $ 39,181
You physically get to make the lenses that people need to see. Also good if you like telescopes or lighting things on fire with a magnifying glass

HEALTHCARE

I don't want to work in a hospital

Chiropractors

| 0.90% | Doctoral or professional degree | $ 72,200

Do you love that feeling when you crack your neck? You do this professionally with all the bones in the body and get paid to do it.

Marriage and Family Therapists

| 21.30% | Master's degree | $ 52,058

Apparently ramming my brother's truck when he ate the last of the Fruit Loops was not an appropriate response. Who knew?

Community Health Workers

| 12.70% | Postsecondary training (non-degree) | $ 40,956

You fight on behalf of patients to make sure that they have access to the health services they need. Like a medical focused lawyer.

Skincare Specialists

| 13.50% | Postsecondary training (non-degree) | $ 34,691

Right between beauty consultant and medical practitioner. They help analyze your skin and give you products and treatments to help you glow.

HEALTHCARE

I want to work in a hospital

Pediatricians
| 8.90% | Doctoral or professional degree | $ 194,376
This kind of doctor works with kids. Always has a lollipop somewhere on them, but also will try to give you a shot.

Nurse Practitioners
Registered Nurses | 29.40% | Master's degree | $ 121,507
These the highest ranking nurses. They have just about as much knowledge as a doctor, but get to spend more time with patients.

Physician Assistants
| 34.70% | Master's degree | $ 119,370
You assist the doctor in whatever the patient needs, as well as help with follow-up and notes. You still get to wear the fancy white coat.

Registered Nurses
Nursing Assistants | 13.40% | Bachelor's degree | $ 98,760
This is like the mini boss of Nursing. extra training and extra skills, but still gets to work directly with patients.

Professional

Professional jobs require a certain amount of training and experience, but offer more defined and expansive career path growth. For example, somebody teaching in a school is probably not going to advance their career much further than that. They might become a department head, but the role they start as is pretty close to the role they'll retire with. As opposed to somebody working at a burger restaurant. They might start off as a fry cook, but that leads to key holder, assistant manager, manager, regional manager, ect...

All the skills, experience, and connections needed to advance are usually baked into the job itself. Someone who is a manager of a store didn't necessarily go to college for management, but their company invested in training them to be one. And those skills and experiences transfer to other areas like retail or sale, especially higher up the corporate ladder. Someone who spent a lot of time in management, project organization, or human resources can find a job at just about any company in any industry.

The down side to all of this is that the goal of just about every company is to make money. No one is going to hand you raises or advancements, and even if your path looks clear you will still have to compete with people who are willing to play dirty. If a company can make more money off of you, they will. It can be a hard balancing act between preserving your sense of self and what's right and advancing in business. But if you can thread that needle, you will have a successful time in the world of business professional careers.

PROFESSIONAL

I want science to be part of my work

Hydrologists
| 6.50% | Bachelor's degree | $ 83,273

You find and trace sources of water, their effect on the land, and how people use them. Kind of like a Waterbender from Avatar.

Environmental Scientists
| 13.40% | Bachelor's degree | $ 83,196

These scientists study the effects of humans on nature. Apparently, grilling salmon in the break room is considered an environmental hazard.

Medical Scientists
| 8.30% | Doctoral or professional degree | $ 80,870

These are the folks that figured out that you should wash your hands to not get sick.

Soil and Plant Scientists
| 9.20% | Bachelor's degree | $ 80,545

These scientists get the 'dirt' on what our Earth is made of, and how we can best use it for growing plants and crops. A good mix of outdoor time and lab work, but always seem to forget to wipe their shoes before coming inside.

PROFESSIONAL

I want science to be part of my work

Sociologists
| 16.70% | Master's degree | $ 120,874

You study how people act in different groups, and then sell that information to TikTok and other companies so that they can make better advertisements.

Atmospheric and Space Scientists
| 14% | Bachelor's degree | $ 105,894

Maybe it's their positive attitude, or maybe it's because they study everything from the weather to the start. Either way, these scientists are always looking up.

Materials Scientists
| 14.80% | Bachelor's degree | $ 104,450

You figure out how to make shoes more bouncy, and cars less bouncy, by analyzing and creating new materials.

Physicists
| 0% | Master's degree | $ 83,326

Physicists figure out the math behind things smashing into other things. That can be waves, explosions, cars, or stars.

PROFESSIONAL

I want science to be part of my work

Epidemiologists
| 5.70% | Doctoral or professional degree | $ 79,346

These are the doctors that study the spread of infectious disease across the population. Yeah right, like that would ever happen... So what did y'all do in 2020?

Biochemists and Biophysicists
| 11% | Master's degree | $ 79,195

These are like biology hackers. They look at how physics and chemicals interact with the natural world and bend it

Conservation Scientists
| 8.40% | Bachelor's degree | $ 78,361

These people make sure that when new developments or farms are built that erosion doesn't make them crumble into the sea. Their job is to improve the land for people while protecting the environment.

Geoscientists, Except Hydrologists and Geographers
| 12.60% | Bachelor's degree | $ 76,112

They study the shape of the world and everything inside of it. They probably love Rubix cubes as well.

PROFESSIONAL

I want to explore the world

Geographers
| 0% | Bachelor's degree | $ 85,959

A job that combines technology and exploration. They study the shape of land and help determine its properties and boundaries for things like maps and land development.

Surveyors
Surveying and Mapping Technicians | 10.90% | Bachelor's degree | $ 73,736

They find exactly where the property lines are so you can build a fence to keep your nosey neighbor out.

Cartographers and Photogrammetrists
| 27.10% | Bachelor's degree | $ 73,387

Both use high tech tools to make maps that include elevation data. Cartographers are one of the oldest professions, but don't say you work in the oldest profession, that's something else.

Foresters
| 4% | Bachelor's degree | $ 72,142

If you drive a Subaru Forester to your job maintaining trees in a forest, does that make you Forester x Forester or Forester^2?

PROFESSIONAL

I want get away from it all

Airline Pilots
| 12.70% | Associate's degree | $ 111,120

You ride inside a big metal bird and make sure it jumps up and down safely.

Commercial Pilots
| 10.90% | Associate's degree | $ 86,391

You fly a big metal bird but instead of it being filled with people, it's filled with little brown boxes.

Flight Attendants
| 18.60% | High school diploma or equivalent | $77,697

Free flights and free peanuts. Who could ask for more.

Locomotive Engineers
| -1.70% | High school diploma or equivalent | $ 75,475

You drive the trains, and if you are lucky you get to meet Thomas the Tank Engine.

PROFESSIONAL

I want to have adoring fans

Athletes and Sports Competitors

| -- | High school diploma or equivalent | $ 77,175

Sure, if you're in the NFL you're going to make millions. But have you thought about being a professional table tennis star? Less money, but less head injuries as well.

Musicians and Singers

| 2.70% | High school diploma or equivalent | $64,480

When singing in the shower just isn't enough.

Writers and Authors

| 4.40% | Bachelor's degree | $ 62,358

They put charcoal on dead trees in the shape of tiny squiggles to make you hallucinate about a story they've created.

Actors

| 10.10% | High school diploma or equivalent | $58,102

"Why, except as a means of livelihood, a man should desire to act on the stage when he has the whole world to act in, is not clear to me."
-George Bernard Shaw

PROFESSIONAL

I want to have Big Boss energy

Chief Executives
| -5.20% | Bachelor's degree | $ 129,109

AKA, the CEO, the Big Boss, the Head Cheese. Is responsible for making the big decisions and leading the executive team in a company.

Lawyers
Paralegals and Legal Assistants | 6.40% | Doctoral degree | $ 116,960

Objection! Conjecture! Conjection! I rest my case.

Captains and Pilots of Water Vessels
| -4.30% | Postsecondary training (non-degree) | $ 74,098

Getting a boat up a river actually takes a lot of skill. It's kind of like memorizing a dance, but with a 1,000 tons of steel.

Lodging Managers
| 12.60% | High school diploma or equivalent | $ 52,070

Works primarily with hotels. You make sure your crew puts a mint on the pillow and keeps the breakfast continental.

PROFESSIONAL

I want to help people at their job

Occupational Health and Safety Specialists

Occupational Health and Safety Techs | 9% | Bachelor's | $ 80,788

They make sure the shelf above you at Home Depot doesn't come crashing down by establishing safety measures for employees.

Arbitrators and Conciliators

| 20.40% | Bachelor's degree | $ 79,546

Sometimes when people argue over who owns the Pokemon cards after a breakup, they hire an Arbitrator to help divide them up. Less expensive and less embarrassing than court.

Training Specialists

| 12.10% | Bachelor's degree | $ 63,741

When a person is hired or promoted , a training specialist helps get them ready for their new job by working with them directly or by making training materials. Kind of like a personal trainer, but with more paperwork.

Human Resources Specialists

| 8.90% | Bachelor's degree | $ 62,160

You work between employees and a company to make sure everybody is happy. Or, as happy as they can be when they are on the clock.

PROFESSIONAL

I want to help people find home

Farm and Home Management Advisors

| 6.50% | Bachelor's degree | $ 75,521

You help people plan their farms and orchards. You also probably always eat your vegetables.

Real Estate Appraiser

| 6% | Postsecondary training (non-degree) | $ 65,463

The best parts of snooping around somebody's home and judging them. You decide how much a house is worth for real estate and tax purposes.

Real Estate Brokers

| 5.60% | Postsecondary training (non-degree) | $ 55,500

You help people buy and sell houses for a percentage of the cost of the house. Usually you don't have a salary, but if you sell big you win big.

Real Estate Sales Agents

| 5.80% | Postsecondary training (non-degree) | $ 42,183

Marge: "Well, like we say: The right house for the right person. Hutz: "Listen, it's time I let you in on a little secret, Marge. The right house is the house that's for sale. The right person is anyone."

PROFESSIONAL

I want to add to perfection

Film and Video Editors
| 14.20% | Associate's degree | $ 55,770

A YouTuber without an editor is just a crazy person ranting in front of a camera.

Editors
| -0.20% | Bachelor's degree | $ 52,262

Sumone who cheks 4 spelling and grammar in riting. Also makes sure the story makes sense in a book,

Costume Attendants
| 9.40% | High school diploma or equivalent | $ 49,693

Sometimes the costumes come alive at night and demand the blood of a seamstress. Other times, they just need an attendant to make sure all the pieces are together and are ready to go.

Fabric Menders, Except Garment
| -- | High school diploma or equivalent | $ 44,134

The reverse of the people who rip holes in your jeans

PROFESSIONAL

I want to make art and a living

Art Directors
| 9.10% | Bachelor's degree | $ 103,727

Art directors keep the feel of a brand or projects consistent

Fashion Designers
| 6.50% | Bachelor's degree | $ 77,270

Why watch Project Runway when you can live it!

Graphic Designers
| 11.60% | Associate's degree | $ 53,709

A great job for an artist who wants something dependable. Graphic designers make everything from food packaging to billboards in Times Square.

Painters, Sculptors, and Illustrators
| 3.70% | High school diploma or equivalent | $ 50,738

"Don't think about making art, just get it done. Let everyone else decide if it's good or bad, whether they love it or hate it. While they are deciding, make even more art."
- Andy Warhol

PROFESSIONAL

I want to make things look good

Interior Designers
| 13.80% | Associate's degree | $ 58,434

The opposite of an exterior decorator. If you tend to watch a lot of design shows and think you could do better, this could be a job for you.

Apparel Patternmakers
| 4.70% | High school diploma or equivalent | $49,680

Ever wish you could clone your favorite jeans? A patternmaker figures out all the puzzle pieces that go into making an article of clothing.

Tailors, Dressmakers, and Custom Sewers
| -0.20% | Less than high school | $ 44,949

I would also add cosplayers to this category. You help people create the outfits that are in their head by picking the right materials, patterns, and sewing styles.

Jewelers
| -2% | Postsecondary training (non-degree) | $41,900

You make everything from wedding rings to tooth grills.

PROFESSIONAL

I want to make the most money

Marketing Managers
| 13.90% | Bachelor's degree | $127,896

They manage all aspects of a promotion, from its design to how many free keychains they give away. Then they track how many of those free keychains turned into actual sales.

Sales Engineers
| 11.70% | Bachelor's degree | $ 119,906

This is the kind of salesperson who sells the big dollar stuff like oil rigs and hospital equipment. Plus you get to schmooze people over fancy meals and charge it to your company.

Sales Managers
| 11.20% | Bachelor's degree | $ 119,050

Manages a team of salespeople and helps them find customers and reach their goals. You usually see them in movies being kind of cranky and smoking a cigar

Financial Managers
| 20.70% | Bachelor's degree | $ 118,230

They track all the "financials" of a company.
When you "take a penny leave a penny", they know.

PROFESSIONAL

I want to manage big projects

Advertising and Promotions Managers

| 11.60% | Bachelor's degree | $ 102,646

These are the people that get to convince their boss that they should fly to Hawaii with their favorite celebrity to film a commercial for Old Spice.

Public Relations and Fundraising Managers

| 10.80% | Bachelor's degree | $ 94,553

Really two different jobs. One does things to make the company look better, the other helps raise money to support the goals of the company or non-profit. Lots of fancy dinners involved.

Operations Research Analysts

| 28.70% | Bachelor's degree | $ 87,808

These are professional problem solvers who use data for complex problems. If you love statistics and telling other people what to do, this would be a great fit.

Budget Analysts

| 7.10% | Bachelor's degree | $ 80,800

Have you ever seen someone's Amazon purchase history and were really judgy about it? This is the job for you.

PROFESSIONAL

I want to manage companie's money

Economists
| 12.30% | Bachelor's degree | $ 97,472

Kind of like a weather forecaster but for money. You advise companies and government agencies about the future financial climate.

Financial Analysts
| 11% | Bachelor's degree | $ 83,905

You tell people and companies how to spend money to make the most profit. Like advising them to buy more copies of this book to help stimulate the economy.

Credit Analysts
| 5.90% | Bachelor's degree | $ 75,624

You help people borrow money so they can be trusted to borrow more money.

Accountants and Auditors
| 10.80% | Bachelor's degree | $ 72,594

Nobody asks you questions when you say you're an accountant (What do you do?) I'm an accountant (Where do you work?) At a place where accountants work (Do you like your job?) Yes, I like my job, and my job is an accountant.

PROFESSIONAL

I want to manage people's money

Personal Financial Advisors
| 8.70% | Bachelor's degree | $ 99,516

You help people figure out what to do with their money in terms of investment and growth. I wonder what they would say about my $42 in savings?

Tax Preparers
| 10.40% | Postsecondary training (non-degree) | $ 50,302

You help people figure out which forms to file, what their income bracket is, and explain that Silly String is not a deductible business expense, even though it should be.

Credit Counselors
| 12.40% | Bachelor's degree | $ 50,098

In this crazy world you have to have credit to get credit. These people help decipher the riddle of the credit card.

Bookkeeping and Auditing Clerks
| -0.40% | Postsecondary training (non-degree) | $ 44,588

Sadly, you don't actually get to keep any books. Instead you track the incoming and outgoing money for a company.

PROFESSIONAL

I want to manage organizations

Compensation and Benefits Managers

| 6.80% | Bachelor's degree | $ 111,038

Pro tip, if someone asks you "how much do you expect to make for this job" say "I've researched the market and with my experience I should be paid above the median market rate for this position".

Purchasing Managers

| 12.40% | Bachelor's degree | $ 107,193

Basically you get to shop everyday. You find the best prices in markets around the world and occasionally go and check out the goods for yourself.

Logisticians

| 11.70% | Bachelor's degree | $ 73,857

You make sure all the finished goods and parts are stored and shipped on time. Like a big industrial ballet.

Manager of Retail Sales Workers

| 3.50% | High school diploma or equivalent | $ 42,801

Beware, these are the people referred to when someone "want to speak to the manager".

PROFESSIONAL

I want to manage other people

Natural Sciences Managers
| 8.90% | Bachelor's degree | $ 115,336

You are kind of the boss nerd in this job. If your company has lots of scientists working to develop a product, you oversee all of them to make sure their lab coats are extra crisp and clean.

Human Resources Managers
| 11.90% | Bachelor's degree | $ 108,848

When Angela fills her office cubicle with cat posters, this is the person you would talk to to get them replaced with the much better dog posters.

Training Managers
| 11.30% | Bachelor's degree | $ 103,299

Someone has to show you how to do your job. They train the people that train people!

Administrative Services Managers
| 10% | Bachelor's degree | $ 97,229

Kind of the big boss secretary. You make sure everything inside of the company run smoothly from the copy

PROFESSIONAL

I want to plan buildings

Urban and Regional Planners
| 13.50% | Bachelor's degree | $ 87,370

Even though cities seem jumbled together, there's actually a lot of planning that goes into the layout. this job is equal parts SimCity and Monopoly.

Architects, Except Landscape and Naval
| 15.80% | Bachelor's degree | $ 80,688

Architects are constantly building and shaping structures in their mind, and then somehow convincing their hands to translate that into images and numbers.

Civil Engineering Technicians
| 9.40% | Associate's degree | $ 73,007

Works with Civil Engineers to make sure everyone stays civil. Helps plan large-scale projects like highways and dams.

Architectural and Civil Drafters
| 7.30% | Postsecondary training (non-degree) | $ 57,832

Works with architects and engineers to draw up and plan their designs. Always has a pencil and protractor with them at all times.

PROFESSIONAL

I want to read and research

Historians
| -- | Master's degree | $ 72,265

Those who don't learn from the past are doomed to repeat it. Those who fail history class are also doomed to repeat it as well. Historians uncover and interpret the past so people can enjoy it in the future.

Technical Writers
| 10.60% | Bachelor's degree | $ 71,878

You write specific instructions on how to do specific things. Perfect job for writers who hate all that creative junk but love to explain how things work.

Interpreters and Translators
| 20.40% | High school diploma or equivalent | $ 58,340

An amazing job for somebody who speaks a second language. You help prepare documents and assist in communication between cultures and languages.

Archivists
| 7.30% | Master's degree | $ 57,600

Did you know there are some oscar-winning films that there are no known copies of? If only an archivist had thought to preserve a copy on something that wouldn't degrade over time.

PROFESSIONAL

I want to make art and a living

Actuaries
| 18.30% | Bachelor's degree | $ 106,514

They research how much risk a new product or service would cost a company. Like the person in a friends group who thinks it's not a good idea to go cliff diving, even if it's "for the 'Gram".

Organizational Psychologists
| 12% | Master's degree | $ 91,019

Figures out how to make employees in a company more happy and efficient. Everything from making sure there's cake on people's birthdays to ordering more comfortable chairs.

Statisticians
Statistical Assistants | 31.30% | Bachelor's degree | $ 79,337

You look at a set of numbers and then change the question so that you always have the right answer. Well, not really, but interpreting data to fit a question is one of their superpowers.

Media Specialist: Education-related
| 8% | High school diploma or equivalent | $ 67,758

Y'all remember when the teacher would set up the TV and you knew it was going to be a good day? This is the person who helped put those shows together

PROFESSIONAL

I want to play with other's money

Gaming Managers
| 16.40% | Associate's degree | $ 72,714

Sadly has nothing to do with video games. You work in casinos to make sure everything goes smoothly.

Market Research Analysts Specialists
| 25.60% | Bachelor's degree | $ 65,236

It's even better than being a trendsetter, it's more like a trend fortune teller.

Insurance Sales Agents
| 4.60% | Postsecondary training (non-degree) | $ 57,112

Kind of like being in the mafia. You go up to someone in a car and say "nice ride, would be a real shame if something happened to it".

Financial Services Sales Agents
| 5% | Bachelor's degree | $ 54,499

You sell services that help manage money. Ironically, these services cost money, which seems counterintuitive, right?

PROFESSIONAL

I want to work in transportation

Motorboat Operators

| 9.10% | High school diploma or equivalent | $ 72,543

Pilots smaller boats for fishing trips, just like the one in Jaws. I'm sure nothing will go wrong...

Avionics Technicians

| 9% | Postsecondary training (non-degree) | $ 67,048

Makes sure all the feathers on those giant metal birds work the way they should. Probably gets to skip security at the airport.

Airfield Operations Specialists

| 8.70% | High school diploma or equivalent | $ 54,486

You get to spend a lot of time near airplanes, but not necessarily in airplanes. You make sure airports and airfields run smoothly.

Aircraft Cargo Handling Supervisors

| 13.80% | High school diploma or equivalent | $ 43,510

You get to supervise my luggage getting lost before a flight.

PROFESSIONAL

I want to work in justice and law

Forensic Science Technicians
| 17.60% | Bachelor's degree | $ 78,896

These are the people on CSI who figure out how and when a person died.

Admin Law Judges
| 7% | Doctoral or professional degree | $ 75,713

You help with the everyday applications of the law. Less intense than supreme court, but people still stand up when you enter the room.

Court Reporters
| 0 | Postsecondary training (non-degree) | $48,266

If you can type faster on your phone then you can speak, this is an amazing career. You type out what people say in a courtroom as cases are being presented.

Judicial Law Clerks
| 5.70% | Doctoral or professional degree | $ 35,331

They work behind the scenes to keep a courtroom moving. What, you think the person with the wooden hammer does all the work?

PROFESSIONAL

I want to work with actual products

Sales Reps for Tech and Science Products
| 11.70% | Bachelor's degree | $ 90,120

If you can sell a brick to somebody building a house, why not sell a brick making machine to somebody who makes skyscrapers?

Commercial and Industrial Designers
| 15.50% | Bachelor's degree | $ 77,217

If you want to be an inventor, this is the career path. You design gadgets and toys that both look cool and work well.

Wholesale Sales Rep
| 9.10% | High school diploma or equivalent | $ 64,035

Maybe not so much these days, but this used to be the 'traveling salesman' kind of job. Lots of phone calls, lots of contracts, and lots of company-paid dinners.

Mechanical Drafters
| 2.20% | Postsecondary training (non-degree) | $ 59,930

The middle step between planning something on paper and making it in production. Good for people who like to go to the grocery store but don't like cooking or picking out recipes.

PROFESSIONAL

I want to work with celebs and artists

Hollywood Agent
| 7% | Bachelor's degree | $ 72,706

The best parts of being in entertainment without being an entertainer. You help people negotiate salaries and contracts for movies, commercials, and product sponsorships.

Public Relations Specialists
| 8.60% | Bachelor's degree | $ 64,180

You know when YouTubers and celebrities do something messed up? This is the team that helps them clean up their image and make those cheesy apology videos.

Public Address System and Other Announcers
| 7.80% | High school diploma or equivalent | $ 43,009

They get to be the big overhead voice at the stadium!

Choreographers
| -- | High school diploma or equivalent | $ 31,021

1,2,3,4, and tap and spin and tap and stop! Now jazz hands! There, you just did choreography for the next big dance.

PROFESSIONAL

I want work with food

Food Scientists and Technologists

| 10.40% | Bachelor's degree | $ 75,114 *Ag/Food Sci Technician*

You know those nutrition facts on the side of Oreos? They

Chefs and Head Cooks

| 12.40% | Postsecondary training (non-degree) | $ 53,696

When you want to be Gordon Ramsay but without the television crew.

Agricultural and Food Science Technicians

| 9.10% | Associate's degree | $ 43,388

You burn Oreos and see how long the flame stays on. After you are done crying over burnt cookies, you send the data to a food scientist for processing and analysis.

Cooks

| 20.70% | Less than high school | $ 32,182

I want the salad on the side. If the salad comes on top, I send it back. Makes good food, occasionally gets yelled at by a celebrity chef.

PROFESSIONAL

Jake B
Lead Brewer

What do you make now compared to the when you started?
19 an hour now, 16 an hour then.

Why did you decide to work in this field and why have you continued to stay?
I like beer, and I like having a job in which I am able to use my creativity to create a product people can enjoy

What career goal are you reaching for right now? How much work will it take and when will you get there?
Head brewer. I would like to be a partner/owner, with partner/s taking care of legal, technical, and financial aspects, so it would take a lot of work and meeting the right people at the right time.

What kind of person would be you ideal co-worker or employee? And who do you wish wouldn't apply?
A hard worker who is organized and has a creative side. Don't apply if you can't multi-task or don't like to get down and dirty.

If money wasn't an issue, would you change careers? If so, what would you do?
I don't think I would change careers, but I would work less hours as it is very physically demanding. If you love beer and don't mind hard work it can be incredibly rewarding.

PROFESSIONAL

I want to work with celebs and artists

TV Camera Operators
A/V Equipment Tech | 11.70% | High school diploma | $ 55,692

Do you know Walmart sells a camera for video production that's $28,000? I would rather take this job and be paid to play with somebody else's expensive equipment than have to buy one on my own.

Meeting, Convention, and Event Planners
| 10.40% | Bachelor's degree | $ 51,649

A really fun job where you get people with a common interest together. Part 'Party Planner' and part salesperson. Usually gets lots of freebies at the end of the convention.

Music Directors and Composers
| 1% | Bachelor's degree | $ 46,883

Did you know Beyonce, Ne-Yo, and Kelly Clarkson have the same composer?

Coaches and Scouts
| 13.60% | High school diploma or equivalent | $ 37,952

If you like the idea of being a lion tamer, but really are more of a people person

PROFESSIONAL

I want to work with quiet customers

Funeral Service Managers
| 10% | Associate's degree | $ 60,330

You help make sure there are plenty of coffins in stock, gas in the hearse, and stones for the tomb.

Embalmers
| -- | Associate's degree | $ 53,368

You help make corpses look pretty so they can say goodbye without scaring the children. Also gets to do makeup on people without hearing any complaints from them.

Morticians and Undertakers
| 12.30% | Associate's degree | $ 43,824

Makes arrangements for funerals. Like that one time in 1998 when The Undertaker threw Mankind off Hell in a Cell, and plummeted sixteen feet through an announcer's table.

Funeral Attendants
| -- | High school diploma or equivalent | $ 32,104

Helps make sure funerals run smoothly. Just make sure you always have a fresh handkerchief to share.

PROFESSIONAL

The Job Graveyard
Jobs that are gone, but not forgotten

Ship Engineers
| -16.30% | High school diploma or equivalent | $ 80,331

Like modern day pirates but without the booty. You maintain and repair ships on the open sea.

Executive Secretaries | -17.20% |
High school diploma or equivalent | $ 61,894

Yikes, another career that is quickly going away. It used to be that somebody would manage a physical calendar and landline phone for an executive. But now we have these magical things called "apps" and "the internet".

Title Examiners and Claims Adjusters
| -8.20% | High school diploma or equivalent | $ 59,267

A neat job that is fading away quickly thanks to digital records. Part historian and part investigator, they trace back the history of a property to see who might have claims of ownership to it.

Travel Agents
| -8.30% | High school diploma or equivalent | $ 43,717

Before there was online travel, you used to have to talk to someone who would organize buying your tickets. Still, they know some special tricks for getting good deals on travel.

PROFESSIONAL

The Job Graveyard
Jobs that are gone, but not forgotten

Photographic Process Worker / Operator
| -20.30% | High school diploma or equivalent | $ 41,995

It's the retro version of digital photos. People actually had to take pictures on film and then drop them off to get turned into images on paper. No selfie checks back in the day.

Printing Press Operators
| -8.60% | High school diploma or equivalent | $ 39,807

Before printers, letters and images had to be made on to stamps and pressed onto paper. Watch out for your fingers!

Radio and Television Announcers
| -18.10% | Bachelor's degree | $ 39,320

I think they call these folks "podcasters" now

Photographers
| -12.30% | High school diploma or equivalent | $ 38,979

Everyone thinks they are a photographer these days. But don't get discouraged! If you love this idea, go for it.

PROFESSIONAL

Whenever I talk to a student about their future and they say "engineer", it sets off my spider-senses. The next questions I ask is "what kind of engineer and why?". 9 times out of 10, they don't have an answer for this. But the truth is there; they want to make money. And like we've said, that is a fine answer, but what will your days look like when you are making that money? Where do you want to spend your time? Who do you want to be around and who do you want to serve?

Below are several different types of engineers and their average pay. Generally, there is only about a 20% difference between the highest salary and the lowest (the exception being the Architecture Manager, which technically still requires engineering training). So if there isn't a huge difference in pay, why not explore a field that is of interest to you?

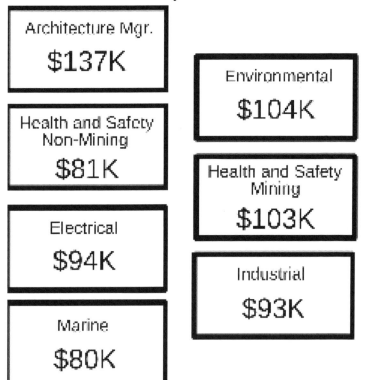

PROFESSIONAL

When thinking about an engineering job, ask yourself questions? Do you want to work indoors or outdoors? Do you want to travel or work near your home? Do you want to make big structures or intricate parts?

Remember, the industry you choose is going to have people who've answered these questions as well. They'll be your co-workers, supervisors, and friends. So don't let an extra few thousand sway you from choosing one job over another. If your daily environment satisfies you, there is more value in that than a couple extra bucks at the end of the month.

That's not to say you shouldn't go for the extra money if it's available. The difference in training between a mining and non-mining safety engineer is negligible, but the difference in pay is almost $2,000 per month!

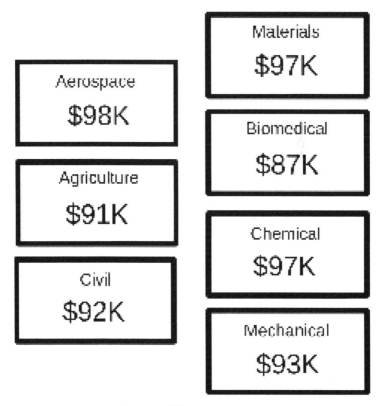

Social Service

Social service jobs make supporting the community one of their primary goals. This can range from law enforcement to education to foresters. Primarily these will be government jobs which come with their own benefits and downsides. Much like professional jobs, there's usually a fairly defined career path.

Unlike more traditional jobs, promotions in these fields are usually based on set written criteria. For example, if somebody works at the post office and wants to move to postmaster, they will need to have worked there for 10 years and have at least a master's degree. This can be less than motivating for people who are driven to move up or have a special talent for their job because advancement does not entirely depend on the quality of their work. So you have to decide whether a sense of security is worth the trade.

For government-backed service jobs, there's less of the motivation for the organization to make profit. This usually means higher wages and better benefits with more stability. Many government jobs are union-backed which adds an extra layer of protection for employees. The downside to all of this is that change can be agonizingly slow. Since everything has to go through multiple layers of approval, even small changes that would make a big difference in productivity can take years. It also means that employees who are under-performing have a lot more protection from being fired. So if your coworkers are slacking and you are feeling the stress from that, there can be very little help and recourse to fix it. If you are somebody who can't stand having a solution in front of them that they can't use, this might not be the career path for you. On the other hand, if you want to walk into a job and know exactly what you're doing that day, and every day after that, social service jobs can be an excellent fit.

It also should seem like helping your community should be one of the first things we talk about. But so often people think that being helpful and doing the right thing means that they have to make sacrifices to their own happiness and success. This is not true. People can make a difference in the lives of others regardless of whether their job is socially focused or not. Sure, a librarian is going to have more chances to educate people than the clerk at 7-Eleven. But at the same time, a manager who takes a risk on training someone for a new and more difficult position can be just as life-changing and transformative as teaching them how to read. I wouldn't be here in my classroom typing this out if it wasn't for people in the professional world taking a chance on me.

It still amazes me that we as a society are still willing to invest in these positions. In Oregon, we spend around $12,000 per student per year on education! That is how much we are willing to take out of our pockets and put towards the benefit of other people, and that is just in one branch of social service. Something to consider when you are looking to climb a mountain. Will your efforts to cut a path through snow and mud make it easier for people to follow in your footsteps? And will it bring you happiness to see the trail you have made?

SOCIAL

I want to be on COPS or CSI

Detectives and Criminal Investigators
| 4.80% | Associate's degree | $ 99,358
You get a discount on those hundred yard rolls of crime scene tape.

Police and Sheriff's Patrol Officers
| 6.60% | High school diploma or equivalent | $ 79,548
You get to ride in the car that goes "wee woo wee woo"

Correctional Officers and Jailers
| -3.10% | High school diploma or equivalent | $ 71,880
If you ever wanted to live out your fantasy of being on a TLC special, this might be the fast track to get there.

Probation Officer and Specialists
| 7.20% | Bachelor's degree | $62,433
A really important part of keeping people out of jail is helping them reenter society. Someone has to be there to help them find an apartment and explain why Squid Game is so popular.

SOCIAL

I want a quiet job

Postmasters and Mail Superintendents

| -1.40% | High school diploma or equivalent | $ 74,520

This is the one person who never gets their package lost in the mail.

Anthropologists and Archaeologists

| 9.70% | Bachelor's degree | $65,372

Lots of digging, lots of discovery, occasional Indiana Jones references. Helps preserve and present the histories of others.

Postal Service Mail Carriers

| 9.30% | High school diploma or equivalent | $50,077

Fresh air, sunshine, lots of walking exercise, and you get to see what all your neighbors are ordering.

Forest Conservation Technicians

| 0.10% | High school diploma or equivalent | $38,019

Pine scented air and paid hiking daily. As long as you have earplugs or are deaf to chainsaws, a perfectly quiet and serene job helping preserve and maintain forests.

SOCIAL

I want to be where the action is!

Air Traffic Controllers
| 3.60% | Postsecondary training (non-degree) | $ 99,372

You get to talk in code to metal birds in the sky to help them land.

Emergency Management Directors
| 7.10% | Bachelor's degree | $ 77,419

In the movies where there's that one person in the button-up shirt with suspenders with a headset on coordinating all the emergency crews? Ya, that's this job.

Police / Fire Dispatchers
| 6.20% | High school diploma or equivalent | $59,043

If you can keep calm in a group chat when drama is going down this is a good career path for you.

Animal Control Workers
| -- | High school diploma or equivalent | $56,458

Half the time you're fighting raccoons in a dumpster, the other half you're rescuing adorable kittens from trees.

SOCIAL

I want to help people's hearts

Healthcare Social Workers
Social / Human Service Assist. | 13.10% | Bachelor's | $ 76,930

You help make sure people have access to affordable health care, no matter their situation. You also probably have a jar of lollipops just like at the doctor's office.

Child, Family, and School Social Workers
| 11% | Bachelor's degree | $52,079

A really important job where you help people in bad situations get the resources they need to live a better life.

Clergy
| 3.40% | Bachelor's degree | $49,610

"Ask your higher power if becoming a minister is right for you. Side effects may include: Waking up early on Sunday mornings, starchy white collars, and choir songs stuck in your head.

Mental Health Substance Abuse Social Workers
| 16.40% | Master's degree | $45,738

People experiencing addiction and substance abuse really need the most patient and compassionate folks to help take care of them. This is a vital job that will change the way you see the world.

SOCIAL

I want to make learning more fun

Instructional Coordinators
| 10.80% | Bachelor's degree | $ 91,560

All the fun of teaching without having to deal with teachers, parents, or students. You review curriculum and see if they're effective at getting students to learn certain objectives.

Librarians
Library Technicians / Assistants | 7.50% | Master's degree |$ 67,758

Way more than books. They are guardians of free speech, privacy laws, information access, and keeping quiet.

Set and Exhibit Designers
| 9.60% | Bachelor's degree | $65,937

Was your favorite assignment making those shoebox dioramas in school? This is the same thing, except a little bit bigger than a shoe box and you probably get to work with artifacts of dinosaur bones.

Curators
Museum Technicians / Conservators | 10.70% | Master's degree | $54,765

You get to decide what pieces of Art and history work well together inside of exhibits and galleries. Perfect if you loved to make giant collages on your walls from posters and magazines.

SOCIAL

I want to make the most money

Judges and Magistrate
| 7.80% | Doctoral or professional degree | $ 149,665

You get a tiny wooden hammer and get to yell "Overruled!"

School Administrators
| 8.30% | Master's degree | $ 113,611

Every time someone says "go to the principal's office", that just means your office.

Manager of Police and Detectives
| 6.40% | High school diploma or equivalent | $ 111,312

You know in the detective shows where the cop does something too extreme and his boss yelled at him to turn in his gun in his badge? That's this job.

Power Distributors and Dispatchers
| 1.10% | High school diploma or equivalent | $ 110,796

If you ever stuck a fork in an electrical outlet and thought that if you held your phone you could charge it at the same time, this might be the job for you. You help manage where the electricity goes from power plants to people's homes.

SOCIAL

I want to see into people's lives

Compliance Officers
| 9% | Bachelor's degree | $ 71,772

Are you a stickler for the rules? This job lets you be as exacting with rules and regulations as you want to be, and you get to punish other people for not doing it as well as you do.

Private Detectives and Investigators
| 7.40% | Associate's degree | $ 67,160

You get to wear a long trench coat and a fedora without looking like a nerd. Though someone might mistake you for McGruff the Crime Dog.

Guidance, School, and Vocational Counselors
| 9.20% | Master's degree | $62,041

If this book was a person, this would be their job. They help people get on track with what they want to do with their futures.

Postal Service Clerks
| 9.30% | High school diploma or equivalent | $51,470

They sell tiny stick-on pictures for envelopes. Combines the best part of working in an assembly line with actually seeing other humans.

SOCIAL

I want to stay in school

Kindergarten Teachers
| 8.40% | Bachelor's degree | $ 77,913

Just in case addition and subtraction are a challenge for you, here you can show off that you know a triangle from a circle.

Elementary School Teachers
Teacher Assistants | 7.70% | Bachelor's degree | $ 71,006

You get to teach a whole bunch of different subjects. And if you're like my grade school art teacher you also get to watch soap operas while the kids are at recess while you drink your tiny milk box. Seems pretty fun.

Middle School Teachers Education
Teacher Assistants | 7.90% | Bachelor's degree | $ 67,442

When you missed out on being a sassy teenager or missed out on yelling at sassy teenagers. Prepare for TikToks and emo music.

Adult Basic Education and Literacy Teachers
| -0.40% | Bachelor's degree | $63,387

This is a really amazing job where you help people who may have had difficulty in school get a little more caught up. It really is a gift to give someone the ability to read.

SOCIAL

I want to work with cool people

Special Education Teachers, Preschool
| 6.80% | Bachelor's degree | $ 86,463

A really great career where you get to work with special needs students before they're even in kindergarten.

Special Education Teachers
| 8.30% | Bachelor's degree | $ 83,108

You work with really cool kiddos help them adjust to school life while giving them the tools they need to be even cooler.

Social / Community Service Managers
| 10.80% | Bachelor's degree | $ 67,624

A cool job where you coordinate big community service projects. Every day is like the big reveal on Extreme Makeover: Home Edition.

Health Educators
| 13.90% | Bachelor's degree | $ 63,465

You teach people how to access different kinds of healthcare and how to do it themselves. Like CPR and first aid trainers. Don't ask Dwight Schrute for help.

SOCIAL

Izzy K.
Graduate Teaching Assistant

What do you make now compared to the when you started?
35k now, expecting 100k+ upon graduation.

Why did you decide to work in this field and why have you continued to stay?
I didn't want to join the workforce yet so I went to grad school so that they would pay me to be in school for six more years.

What career goal are you reaching for right now?
I'm working towards a Math PhD. It should take two more years (six total).

What would you say to someone wanting join your industry?
You'll make a lot of money, it's mostly enjoyable, and it's really not that much work. You'll have to study a lot, but the time will pass anyway and it's super cool to get paid to go to school. Technically I get paid for teaching, but that really only takes up like 5 hours a week and the rest of the time I think about it as being paid to study something I'm interested in.

Who would be your ideal co-worker or employee?
My ideal coworker would actually cares about teaching, but even if you don't you can fake it til you make it and get your degree. Anyone should apply, but I wouldn't want to work with super judgmental people.

SOCIAL

I want to work with fire!

Fire Inspectors and Investigators

| 5.80% | *Postsecondary training (non-degree)* | $ 102,774

When they walk up to a suspicious burnt down house and the police say "what do you think caused it" you get to say "well, I think fire". they are more asking if it was arson, but you get the joke.

Supervisor of Fire Fighting Workers

| 6.60% | *High school diploma or equivalent* | $ 101,977

You get the best seat in the fire truck, the comfiest bunk in the house, and the poll you go down has the best slide.
Oh, you also put out fires.

Firefighters

| 7.60% | *Postsecondary training (non-degree)* | $ 66,568

You don't actually get to fight with fire, which was disappointing to find out

Forest Fire Inspectors and Prevention

| 23.90% | *High school diploma or equivalent* | $58,095

I don't know who made forests out of burnable wood, but your job would be to prevent the most flammable substance on Earth from doing what it does naturally.

Technology

Think about an artist who wants to make a living as an illustrator. Where they were born and where they lived would influence their success more than anything else. A bad illustrator in New York was going to get more work and attention than a genius living in Beloit, Kansas. For most of human history this has just been a fact; your fate was tied to your geography. Now that artist can stand on equal footing no matter where in the world they are. All of this because some folks 50 years ago wanted to send each other a letter without using a stamp.

When people think about tech jobs, they tend to think about the working conditions and the high salaries first. It's true that these are important things to consider. With relatively little higher education, a person can be making six figures from their desk in a field that may never stop growing. What stops a lot of people from entering the world of technology is that they think it's boring or doesn't make a difference. But have you ever had a relative call tech support for a computer issue? Someone had to make the software that let the agent at the call center connect to the user's computer, somebody had to make the training to help the agent figure out what's wrong with that computer, and somebody had to develop the encryption so the credit card payment for the service couldn't get stolen. That is a lot of "sombodys" just to get grandpa on Facebook to show off his bird watching photos. But to him, it might be the only way he can connect with his family.

Even if you are less human focused, the amount of data that we are producing, organizing, and analyzing is tremendous. Think about every book, painting, receipt, and spreadsheet made in all of history. Think all the way back to ancient Egyptians and Mesopotamians and all the scrolls and carvings they made, even the ones that were destroyed over time. Now go all the way from there to 2003 and imagine every piece of data created in a giant library. We, as humans in 2021, make as much data in 2 days as we have made in the previous 5,000 years. If you take 2 days to read this book, as much information will have been created to fill a library the same size as the prior 5 millenia! A big branch of technology jobs are sorting, organizing, and interpreting that new data. A computer still can't understand why it does what we ask it to do. For example, we can run DNA through a computer and have the whole genome mapped out. But it still takes a human to understand the connection between someone getting sick all the time and a string of letters and numbers that a computer spits out. A database can show that certain zip codes have a higher amount of violent crime, but it takes a human to match that to education spending and access to healthy food. So when the government wants to improve the living situation in those areas, they know that education and nutrition are going to have a bigger impact than increased law enforcement.

The future of the world is dependent on technology. Everything from entertainment to climate change are interwoven in this relatively new way we communicate and live. It's almost like every job in technology is part of this interconnected net, like some kind of inter-net.

TECHNOLOGY

I want to make the most money

Computer Systems Managers
| 14.90% | Bachelor's degree | $ 132,363

Yo dawg I heard you like managing computers So we made you manager of the managers who manage the computers.

Computer Research Scientists
| 36.70% | Doctoral or professional degree | $ 120,970

It's like if you were Isaac Newton, but also obsessed with getting more speed out of your Nintendo. Lots of researching and inventing new computer processes and hardware.

Computer Hardware Engineers
| 12.10% | Bachelor's degree | $ 114,176

They are the ones who trick rocks into thinking by feeding them lightning. In other words, they design circuits and other electronics

Computer Network Architects
| 7.40% | Bachelor's degree | $ 113,387

These are the people that figure out how to give everybody a login in a computer network, but also make sure that Roblox is blocked.

Dustin G.
Web Development

What do you make now compared to the when you started?
Started at $50k as a Web Developer with a bump to $60k after a job change, then $80k with a promotion to senior developer, then up to $112 with raises over the years, and currently at $135k after a promotion to managing the development team.

Why did you decide to work in this field and why have you continued to stay?
I started building personal web pages when I was really young and fell in love with all of the little problems there were to solve. I got into my current company when it was young and it's been very exciting to grow along with it. Now I manage a great team maintaining a large public facing website for a publicly traded company

Would you ever consider changing careers?
I would consider it. I've always enjoyed making things with my hands and have dived deeply into woodworking. If I could make the same money, I would consider doing that full time as it is incredibly satisfying seeing people want the things that I make.

What would you say to someone wanting join your industry?
The internet is only going to keep growing, and there are a lot of opportunities for people willing to learn how to build it. If you enjoy innovation and problem solving, this is a fantastic industry.

TECHNOLOGY

I don't want to deal with people

Systems Software Developer

| 13.10% | Bachelor's degree | $ 107,065

They make the serious kinds of software that you usually can't see. Things like hospital systems, military applications, and that smart fridge that nobody bought.

Database Administrators

| 12.30% | Bachelor's degree | $ 103,505

Someone has to build the system that keeps track of all your 7-Eleven reward points. I mean, are you going to track how many Slurpees you drank in the last year?

Network and Systems Administrators

| 5.80% | Bachelor's degree | $ 88,418

You are like the office Santa Claus. You see what people are doing even in incognito mode, you block the naughty websites, and you reward good workers with fancier computers.

Computer Programmers

| -6.20% | Bachelor's degree | $ 86,526

These are kind of like the mechanics of code. They help programs work more efficiently and make those updates that you always ignore.

TECHNOLOGY

I don't want to code

Information Security Analysts
| 31.80% | Bachelor's degree | $ 105,727

You know when your grandma sends you a suspicious email and you have to tell her she never actually won the Mexican Lottery? It's like that, but a career.

Computer Systems Analysts
| 7.70% | Bachelor's degree | $ 100,433

If you like going to trade shows and having sales people shmooze you, this is a pretty good position. You help companies figure out what stuff they need for their systems.

Electrical and Electronics Drafters
| 9.30% | Postsecondary training (non-degree) | $ 68,493

These folks make the drawings in the plans for how a circuit is actually assembled. It comes out looking like something between Egyptian hieroglyphics and a puzzle from Zelda.

Computer Network Support Specialists
| 11% | Bachelor's degree | $ 60,402

These are the people you hope don't show up to work when your network is down and you have a project due in 20 minutes. Because somehow inevitably they'll fix the network with just enough time for you not to have an excuse.

TECHNOLOGY

I don't want to work in an office

Numerical Tool Programmers

| 32.40% | Postsecondary training (non-degree) | $ 61,067

You feed math into a giant machine that then uses a big cutter to carve everything from art to car parts.

Telecom Line Installers

| 12.60% | High school diploma or equivalent | $ 51,579

"I am a lineman for the county, And I drive the main road, Searchin' in the sun for another overload. I hear you singing in the wire, I can hear you through the whine, And the Wichita lineman is still on the line."

PC Machine Tool Operators

| 0.60% | High school diploma or equivalent | $ 44,229

These are the people who use robotics to make the things we all use. When the robots do take over, they will become the butlers for our glorious robot overlords.

Sound Engineering Technicians

| 11.20% | Postsecondary training (non-degree) | $ 42,355

You know when you see one of those recording studios with the big board and all the switches and dials. Ya, I think they don't do anything, I think they are just for show.

TECHNOLOGY

I want to make video games

Software Developers, Applications
| 28.20% | Bachelor's degree | $ 107,065

These are the folks that make everything from video games to tax accounting software. Now if somebody could just combine the two into one program

Multimedia Artists and Animators
| 8.10% | Bachelor's degree | $ 100,594

Did you know the original Toy Story was almost lost because of a computer crash? Luckily, one of the animators working from home had a backup copy. True story!

Web Developers
| 14.40% | Bachelor's degree | $ 78,215

You make the pretty websites that travel through a series of tubes to get to your computer. Usually you get to work with marketing agencies and other creative folks.

Producers and Directors
| 5.90% | Bachelor's degree | $ 63,081

They do all of the behind-the-scenes work to assemble the cast and crew for movies and TV shows. You get to boss around celebrities, so that's a plus.

TECHNOLOGY

The Tech Graveyard

Jobs that are gone, but not forgotten

Computer Operators
| -20% | High school diploma or equivalent | $ 86,328

Thanks to automation, this position has almost disappeared. They would do things like install updates and perform backups.

Word Processors and Typists
| -31.90% | High school diploma or equivalent | $ 41,163

Nobody is typing anymore. I'm not even typing anymore. Why did I just buy $100 keyboard? Oh right, it lights up and looks cool.

Telemarketers
| -16.40% | Less than high school | $ 39,655

We have been trying to contact you about your car's extended warranty. Your car may be eligible for reduced student loan payments if you call now.

Data Entry Keyers
| -21.10% | High school diploma or equivalent | $ 37,357

Yikes, another job we are losing to the robots. There's a lot less demand for transferring information from paper to computers than there used to be.

Trades

Wherever you are right now, think about the people who ran the power lines through your house, brought water to your kitchen sink, and built the roof that you are under. Think of the people who made the roads that brought in those supplies, the drivers that delivered them, and the folks who put up the cell towers that helped coordinate all the work. You, right now, are surrounded by the efforts of dozens of tradespeople who all took part in giving you the moment you are having right now. People whose names you probably will never know and whose efforts you may have never seen. Now think about what your hands might do tomorrow, and the lives you will impact with your labor as a tradesperson. Sounds pretty cool, right?

Trades are mostly defined as jobs that require some kind of specialized skill or education and lean toward physical labor. People sometimes have a false notion that because trade jobs involve using the body, anybody should be able to do it given the right tools. It's unfortunate that across human history, any job that makes you sweat, that makes noise or debris, or that works with waste or garbage, was often considered inferior. And yet without people in the skill professions we would be living out in the wild without protection, sanitation, or comfort.

For the same reasons people discriminate against trade jobs make them a great choice for a lot of people. Most of these jobs have on-site training either through apprenticeship or being an assistant. At the entry level there's often no formal education requirement, it's approachable to people who may not have done well in a school environment. That's not to say these jobs are taken just out of convenience. There's a joy to making something with your own two hands. Even compared to art and technology where you may be making a "something", it's not the same as a house or a road or a hospital. The difficulty may be that often the trade you start off with is the trade you will do for most of your life. The skills and tools from one trade might not apply to another. If someone gets burnt out in one trade path, it can be difficult to start all over again as an apprentice in another. Work hours can be long, stretching from early in the morning to late at night depending on the work. On-call people have to be ready to work at a moment's notice if their income depends on being available at any time to do a repair or service.

There's also a physical toll on the body. Trade jobs are more prone to workplace accidents and injuries, and require more physical work than most other jobs. Without a clear plan towards savings and retirement, a person can get trapped in a job they no longer want or can do. The pay can also be highly variable depending on workplace conditions. A union contractor working on an industrial job site is going to be paid much more than a local contractor working on an off-the-books project. Being independent might make you more money, but it means knowing how to manage a business at the same time as working your trade.

That all being said, people find the work to be satisfying. At the end of the day, you've put your hands to something that people may never know you worked on, but that impacts their lives every day.

TRADES

I want to every day to be different

Explosives Workers and Blasters

| 0 | High school diploma or equivalent | $ 52,175

If you really, really, really like the 4th of July, this is a good job for you. You blow up old buildings for demolition, mountains for mining, and even loose snow about ski resorts.

Earth Drillers, Except Oil and Gas

| 7.20% | High school diploma or equivalent | $ 52,175

I used to watch the prairie dogs build these giant underground burrows. Earth drillers do the same thing, but without having to use their claws and teeth.

Sailors and Marine Oilers

| -5.70% | Less than high school | $ 47,821

Ships have a lot of moving parts, and you don't want them rusting up in the giant salty bathtub of the ocean. Marine oilers keep people from ending us shipwrecked on a desert island.

Automotive Body and Related Repairers

| 7.90% | High school diploma or equivalent | $ 44,172

You can tell people you work at The Body Shop, but that you don't sell lotion or perfume. Instead you fix

TRADES

I want to be judgy

Construction and Building Inspectors

| 10.90% | High school diploma or equivalent | $ 75,513

Do you go "Ummmm, actually" and then correct people on something that they are saying wrong? This is the same thing, but with entire buildings.

Refuse and Recyclable Material Collectors

| 11.50% | Less than high school | $ 48,656

When a building is demolished, these people recycle as much as possible, from the pipes to the cement. And they always steal my soda cans!

Log Graders and Scalers

| 0 | High school diploma or equivalent | $ 47,781

How much wood could a wood judge judge if a wood judge could judge wood?

Agricultural Inspectors

| 5.30% | Bachelor's degree | $ 42,121

Someone has to put that fancy FDA stamp on the food. You get to inspect the quality of produce and feed coming from farms.

TRADES

I want to build buildings

Riggers
| 11.70% | High school diploma or equivalent | $ 62,346

You type things up and lift them in the air. Kind of like a low-budget Spider-Man.

Glaziers
| 11.10% | High school diploma or equivalent | $ 60,576

Disappointingly has nothing to do with donuts. Instead to do something with installing windows. I'm sure there's more to it, I'm just disappointed donuts aren't involved.

Drywall and Ceiling Tile Installers
Construction Laborers | 4% | Less than high school | $ 58,316

The Hipster exposed brick look only works in so many places. This job gives us nice clean walls and ceilings to put fake brick over.

Brickmasons and Blockmasons
Construction Trades' Helpers | 8.80% | H.S.D. or equivalent | $ 57,899

An upgrade from being a sandwichmason, but less delicious. You assemble structures out of bricks and blocks, probably not Legos.

TRADES

I want to build buildings

Carpenters
Carpenter's Helpers | 10% | H.S.D. or equivalent | $ 54,332

They build the buildings. Handy if you have a lot of land, wood, and time on your hands.

Cement Masons and Concrete Finishers
Construction Trades' Helpers | 11.30% | Less than H.S.| $ 53,806

The most advanced version of a kid who likes to play in mud. You build and finish concrete and masonry.

HVAC Mechanics and Installers
| 13.70% | Postsecondary training (non-degree) | $ 53,653

The final warriors on the battle of global warming. Soon, we will all live in giant refrigerators. Installs heating, air conditioning, and other things that make living comfortable.

Plasterers and Stucco Masons
Construction Laborers | 0 | Less than high school | $ 50,852

These folks do all the fancy and interesting designs on the inside and outside of houses with clay and plaster.

TRADES

I want to build buildings

Roofers
Construction Laborers | 9.60% | Less than high school | $ 50,188

The roof, the roof, the roof is on fire!

Tile and Marble Setters
Construction Trades' Helpers | 22.50% | Less than HS| $ 49,657

Ancient Greeks to Soviet Russians would make massive mosaics out of tile and marble stone. Now, it's mostly showers and kitchens.

Carpet Installers
Construction Laborers | 0.10% | Less than high school | $ 49,573

These folks always shock people with static electricity. But they also keep our feet warm. Seems like a fair trade.

Pipelayers
| 8.60% | High school diploma or equivalent | $ 48,393

Kind of a pre-plumber. Pipelayers lay out and install all of the different types of pipe in a construction or renovation project.

TRADES

I want to have more power!

Electricians
Electrician's Helper | 10.60% | H.S.D. or equivalent | $ 80,365

Your job is to make sure all the lightning we have running through the metal snakes in our walls doesn't make our hair stand up.

Wind Turbine Service Technicians
| 0 | Associate's degree | $ 59,515

Did you ever speak into a fan see your voice sounds like a robot? Imagine doing it a thousand feet in the air with a fan the size of an airplane wing.

Cellular Tower Equipment Installers
| 5.50% | Postsecondary training (non-degree) | $ 58,719

These are the secret Illuminati folks that install the 5G on the cell phone towers to control our brains and Instagram feeds... I've already said too much...

Telecommunications Line Installers
| 12.60% | High school diploma or equivalent | $ 51,579

"I am a lineman for the county, And I drive the main road, Searchin' in the sun for another overload. I hear you singing in the wire, I can hear you through the whine, And the Wichita lineman is still on the line."

TRADES

Alexis C.
Barber

Why did you decide to work in this field and why have you continued to stay?

I've always been creative. Growing up, my mom couldn't afford for us to go to the salon/barbershop. We mostly got home cuts and box color. When I got into my teenage years, I started coloring my own hair and keeping up with the trends, then eventually creating my own trends. Eventually my friends started asking me to do their hair, they loved my ideas so much. After trying business degrees and history degrees, I realized I wasn't doing what I loved, only what people told me would be a good job. I wanted to do what I loved, or at least try it out. So I signed up for hair school and I've been doing hair, professionally, for ten years now. Hair is never the same, it is always changing and evolving. I never get bored.

If money wasn't an issue, would you change careers?

I don't think I would, honestly! Hair design keeps me challenged and I get to meet many wonderful people who walk down different paths of life. Maybe I would also study psychology and become a therapist so I can do a combo of hair and therapy! Because sometimes I feel like a therapist already when my clients open up about their lives.

Right now I am working towards opening my own mobile hair business. It's been a lot of work figuring out what legal proceedings I need to follow, what licenses I need, and raising the money to branch off on my own. Hoping to have this business up and running within a year and a half.

Who would be your ideal co-worker or employee?

My ideal coworkers are people who are self-sufficient. Who comes to work ready to greet the day. Who have goals and work actively to meet them. Who continue to seek out more education. And who loves to laugh. The hair business can be tough; lousy customers, expensive tools, slow days. I like people that roll with the punches and celebrate the good days.

TRADES

I want to make the most money

Elevator Installers and Repairers

| 10.30% | High school diploma or equivalent | $ 101,690

Make things go up, make things go down, make sure it doesn't end up looking like a horror movie scene.

Labor Relations Specialists

| -2% | Bachelor's degree | $ 101,492

The "middle man" between the bosses, the companies, and the workers. Always has that "win-win" attitude.

Industrial Production Managers

| 9.10% | Bachelor's degree | $ 97,187

You supervise and manage big scale factories and projects. you probably get to order big tools like bulldozers, so that's fun.

Metal and Plastic Patternmakers

| 0 | High school diploma or equivalent | $ 80,311

You lay out and make the patterns for parts. Kind of like doing a jigsaw puzzle with power tools.

TRADES

I want to make people's day better

Barbers
| 0 | Postsecondary training (non-degree) | $ 47,230

In ancient times, barbers used to pull teeth as well. Maybe it's time we bring that back and save some money from the dentists.

Locksmiths and Safe Repairers
| -3.70% | High school diploma or equivalent | $ 45,961

You don't get to do a lot of safecracking, but you do save a lot of keys locked in cars. So that's kinda like cracking a

Home Appliance Repairers
| 1.50% | High school diploma or equivalent | $ 45,511

This is who you call when your cousin drops too many forks in the garbage disposal.

Pest Control Workers
| 0 | High school diploma or equivalent | $ 42,759

If something is really bugging you this is a great way to get rid of those feelings.

TRADES

I want to plan and organize projects

Supervisors / Managers of Construction Trades
| 11.40% | High school diploma or equivalent | $ 76,076

You get to drink a lot of coffee and wear a hard hat and an orange vest. I think you also manage people as well, but I'm really in it for the coffee.

Landscape Architects
| 11.40% | Bachelor's degree | $ 68,553

If you watch enough HGTV you'll know exactly what this is. You design a plan to transform a dry patch of land can transform into a lush garden.

Industrial Engineering Tech
| 0 | Associate's degree | $ 61,909

When the boss engineer has a really good idea and you have to figure out how to make it actually work.

Geo and Petroleum Technicians
| 0 | Associate's degree | $ 54,448

Oregon doesn't let us pump our own gas. This job pumps it out of the earth, which is pretty much the same thing.

TRADES

I want to work in nature

Fallers and Buckers
| 0 | High school diploma or equivalent | $ 68,187

TIMBERRRRRRRRRR! These folks trim and prepare fresh logs. Lots of pine-scented air.

Environmental Engineering Tech
| 6.90% | Associate's degree | $ 66,234

Do you really like recycling but wish you could do more? These folks literally clean the rivers and restore the land. As close as you'll get to being Capitan Planet.

Tree Trimmers and Pruners
| 12.20% | High school diploma or equivalent | $ 55,577

You make big trees a little bit smaller to keep them healthy and looking good, but there are no prunes involved.

Grounds Maintenance Workers
| 10.40% | Less than high school | $ 34,673

The best parts of being clean and organized combined with being outdoors all day.

TRADES

I want to work on big machines

Rail Car Repairers
| 16.50% | High school diploma or equivalent | $ 72,561

Did you play with trains as a kid? All the fun of playing with them, without having to drive them to the middle of nowhere.

Rail-Track Laying and Maintenance
| 10.70% | High school diploma or equivalent | $ 67,573

You know when Wylie Coyote paints the train tracks into a brick wall? You have that kind of power in this job, but should probably use real tunnels instead.

Aircraft Assemblers
| 0 | High school diploma or equivalent | $55,501

You assemble airplanes and get them ready to fly, but I don't think you get unlimited peanuts like the passengers do.

Farm Equipment Mechanics
| 9.20% | High school diploma or equivalent | $ 53,058

You can take a ride on my big green tractor...as soon as the Farm Equipment Mechanic fixes it.

TRADES

I want to work with metal

Sheet Metal Workers
| 10.70% | High school diploma or equivalent | $ 56,697

If heavy metal is too heavy to listen to, try this.
Sheet metal is the smooth jazz of the metal world.
I think you also make things out of sheets of metal.

Machinists
| 11.80% | High school diploma or equivalent | $ 53,443

Not someone made out of made out of machines. Instead, someone who machines (kind of like carving) parts and tools.

Welders, Cutters, Solderers, and Brazers
| 12.40% | High school diploma or equivalent | $ 49,172

All these jobs use a fire breathing wand to cut, melt, and fuse metal. Like a half dragon and half wizard.

Pourers and Casters
| 6.30% | High school diploma or equivalent | $ 46,430

I was a disappointed to find out that "Caster" did not mean magic caster. Instead it's the person who pours molten metal into a mold to make a shape, which is still pretty cool.

TRADES

I want to work on engines

Bus and Truck Engine Specialists
| 9.10% | High school diploma or equivalent | $ 52,901

Who wants to work on tiny Toyota engines when you can be working on vehicles the size of a small house. Plus, biodiesel engines smell like french fries!

Motorboat Mechanics
| 7.10% | High school diploma or equivalent | $ 45,642

Kind of like a car mechanic, except with no wheels and more water.

Automotive Service Mechanics
| 2.50% | Postsecondary training (non-degree) | $ 45,352

It's kind of like being a doctor to giant metal buffalo.

Motorcycle Mechanics
| 7.60% | High school diploma or equivalent | $ 42,053

You would think it should be half the work of car mechanics, but it's not.

TRADES

I want to work on roads

Equipment Operators
| 10.20% | High school diploma or equivalent | $ 60,531

Get to drive and use all the really big toys. Bulldozers, wrecking balls, and all the other stuff they won't let me on.

Paving, Surfacing, and Tamping Operators
| 11.70% | High school diploma or equivalent | $ 59,176

Nobody likes construction but everybody likes the feel of a fresh new road. This job make sure the roads are level, have a good layer of pavement, and then "tamp" or press it all down together.

Highway Maintenance Workers
| 8.10% | High school diploma or equivalent | $ 55,441

If someone tells you "It's my way or the highway" now it can be both.

Flagger
| 2.30% | Less than high school | 34,220

Helps direct traffic and stops me on road trips long enough to make a sandwich from my driver's seat.

TRADES

I want to work on the road

Bus Drivers, Transit and Intercity

| 8.10% | High school diploma or equivalent | $ 51,260

I knew someone who when they were little thought "catch a bus" meant literally catch-a-bus. They caught it, and it dragged them half a block. They came out fine, by the way.

Truck Drivers, Heavy and Tractor-Trailer

| 9.10% | Postsecondary training (non-degree) | $ 50,379

I really like truck stop food. And there is always a little section in the truck stop for professional truckers. If you have this job, you have a VIP pass across the country to this section.

Truck Drivers, Light or Delivery Services

| 14.50% | High school diploma or equivalent | $ 39,150

You don't have to try to get your 18-wheeler unstuck from a tight intersection. In general you'll just have the standard 4-wheelers to get stuck in

Taxi Drivers and Chauffeurs

| 24.60% | Less than high school | $ 37,795

Imagine if there was a service like Lyft or Uber except, like, The company owned the cars and let you drive them and, like, they were all yellow like that Coldplay song.

INDEX

A

Actors 69
Actuaries 84
Adjusters, Title Examiners and Claims 94
Administrators, Database 115
Administrators, Network and Systems 115
Administrators, School 105
Advisors, Farm and Home Management 72
Advisors, Personal Financial 79
Agent, Hollywood 89
Agents, Financial Services Sales 85
Agents, Insurance Sales 85
Agents, Real Estate Sales 72
Agents, Travel 94
Analysts, Budget 77
Analysts, Computer Systems 116
Analysts, Credit 78
Analysts, Financial 78
Analysts, Information Security 116
Analysts, Operations Research 77
Anesthetists, Nurse 47
Animators, Multimedia Artists and 118
Announcers, Public Address System and Other 89
Announcers, Radio and Television 95
Applications 118
Appraiser, Real Estate 72
Archeologists, Anthropologists and 101
Architects 82
Architects, Computer Network 113
Architects, Landscape 131
Archivists 83
Assemblers, Aircraft 133
Assistants, Medical 56
Assistants, Physician 62
Attendants, Costume 73
Attendants, Flight 68
Attendants, Funeral 93
Audiologists 53
Auditors, Accountants and 78
Authors, Writers and 69

B

Barbers 130
Biologists, Zoologists and Wildlife 50
Biophysicists, Biochemists and 66
Blasters, Explosives Workers and 122
Blockmasons, Brickmasons and 124
Brazers, and 134
Brokers, Real Estate 72
Buckers, Fallers and 132

C

Carpenters 125
Carriers, Postal Service Mail 101
Casters, Pourers and 134
Child 103
Chiropractors 61
Choreographers 89

INDEX

Clergy 103
Clerks, Bookkeeping and Auditing 79
Clerks, Judicial Law 87
Clerks, Postal Service 106
Collectors, Refuse and Recyclable Material 123
Competitors, Athletes and Sports 69
Composers, Music Directors and 92
Conciliators, Arbitrators and 71
Controllers, Air Traffic 102
Convention 92
Cooks 90
Cooks, Chefs and Head 90
Coordinators, Instructional 104
Counselors 55
Counselors, and Vocational 106
Counselors, Credit 79
Counselors, Genetic 53
Counselors, Rehabilitation 58
Curators 104
Cutters 134

D

Dentists 47
Designers, Commercial and Industrial 88
Designers, Fashion 74
Designers, Graphic 74
Designers, Interior 75
Designers, Set and Exhibit 104
Detectives, Manager of Police and 105
Developers, Software 118
Developers, Web 118
Developer, Systems Software 115
Directors, Art 74
Directors, Emergency Management 102
Directors, Producers and 118
Dispatchers, Police / Fire 102
Dispatchers, Power Distributors and 105
Drafters, Architectural and Civil 82
Drafters, Electrical and Electronics 116
Drafters, Mechanical 88
Dressmakers 75
Drillers, Earth 122
Drivers, Bus 137
Drivers, Truck 137
Driver, Taxi 137

E

Economists 78
Editors 73
Editors, Film and Video 73
Education, Middle School Teachers 107
Education-related, Media Specialist: 84
Educators, Health 108
Electricians 127
Embalmers 93
Engineers, Biomedical 54
Engineers, Computer Hardware 113
Engineers, Locomotive 68
Engineers, Sales 76
Engineers, Ship 94

INDEX

Epidemiologists 66
Executives, Chief 70

F

Family 103
Finishers, Cement Masons and Concrete 125
Firefighters 110
Flagger 136
Foresters 67

G

Garment, Except 73
Gas, Except Oil and 122
General 47
Geographers 67
Geographers, Except Hydrologists and 66
Geoscientists 66
Glaziers 124
Guidance 106
Gynecologists, Obstetricians and 47

H

Historians 83
Hydrologists 64
Hygienists, Dental 56

I

Illustrators, and 74
Inspectors, Agricultural 123
Inspectors, Construction and Building 123
Installers, Carpet 126
Installers, Cellular Tower Equipment 127
Installers, Drywall and Ceiling Tile 124
Installers, HVAC Mechanics and 125
Installers, Telecom Line 117
Installers, Telecommunications Line 127
Intercity, Transit and 137
Investigators, Detectives and Criminal 100
Investigators, Fire Inspectors and 110
Investigators, Private Detectives and 106

J

Jailers, Correctional Officers and 100
Jewelers 75
Judges, Admin Law 87

K

Keyers, Data Entry 119

L

Lawyers 70
Librarians 104
Logisticians 80

M

Machinists 134
Magistrate, Judges and 105
Maintenance, Rail-Track Laying and 133
Managers, Administrative Services 81
Managers, Advertising and

140

INDEX

Promotions 77
Managers, Compensation and Benefits 80
Managers, Computer Systems 113
Managers, Financial 76
Managers, Funeral Service 93
Managers, Gaming 85
Managers, Human Resources 81
Managers, Industrial Production 129
Managers, Lodging 70
Managers, Marketing 76
Managers, Medical and Health Services 49
Managers, Natural Sciences 81
Managers, Public Relations and Fundraising 77
Managers, Purchasing 80
Managers, Sales 76
Managers, Social / Community Service 108
Managers, Training 81
Masons, Plasterers and Stucco 125
Mechanics, Automotive Service 135
Mechanics, Farm Equipment 133
Mechanics, Motorboat 135
Mechanics, Motorcycle 135
Meeting 92
Menders, Fabric 73
Microbiologists 50
Midwives, Nurse 57

N

Naval, Except Landscape and 82
Nurses, Licensed Practical and Licensed Vocational 57
Nurses, Registered 62
Nutritionists, Dietitians and 53

O

Officer, Probation 100
Officers, Compliance 106
Officers, Police and Sheriff's Patrol 100
Oilers, Sailors and Marine 122
Operators, and Tamping 136
Operators, Computer 119
Operators, Equipment 136
Operators, Motorboat 86
Operators, PC Machine Tool 117
Operators, Photographic Process Workers 95
Operators, Printing Press 95
Operators, TV Camera 92
Optician, Dispensing 60
Optometrists 60

P

Painters 74
Paramedics, Emergency Medical Tech / 57
Pathologists, Speech-Language 55
Patternmakers, Apparel 75
Patternmakers, Metal and Plastic 129
Paving 136
Pediatricians 62
Pharmacists 52
Phlebotomists 56

INDEX

Photogrammetrists, Cartographers and 67
Photographers 95
Physicists 65
Physiologists, Exercise 59
Pilots, Airline 68
Pilots, Commercial 68
Pipelayers 126
Planners, and Event 92
Planners, Urban and Regional 82
Podiatrists 52
Practitioners, Family and General 47
Practitioners, Nurse 62
Preparers, Medical Equipment 54
Preparers, Tax 79
Preschool 108
Prevention, Forest Fire Inspectors and 110
Products, Sales Reps for Tech and Science 88
Programmers, Computer 115
Programmers, Numerical Tool 117
Prosthetists, Orthotists and 54
Pruners, Tree Trimmers and 132
Psychiatrists 52
Psychologists, Clinical / Counseling / School 58
Psychologists, Organizational 84

R

Repairers, Automotive Body and Related 122
Repairers, Elevator Installers and 129
Repairers, Home Appliance 130
Repairers, Locksmiths and Safe 130
Repairers, Medical Equipment 54
Repairers, Rail Car 133
Reporters, Court 87
Rep, Wholesale Sales 88
Riggers 124
Roofers 126

S

Scalers, Log Graders and 123
School 106
Scientists, Atmospheric and Space 65
Scientists, Computer Research 113
Scientists, Conservation 66
Scientists, Environmental 64
Scientists, Materials 65
Scientists, Medical 64
Scientists, Soil and Plant 64
Scouts, Coaches and 92
Sculptors 74
Secretaries, Executive 94
Services, Light or Delivery 137
Setters, Tile and Marble 126
Sewers, and Custom 75
Singers, Musicians and 69
Sociologists 65
Solderers 134
Sonographers, Diagnostic Medical 53
Specialists, Airfield Operations 86

INDEX

Specialists, and 100
Specialists, Computer Network Support 116
Specialists, Engine 135
Specialists, Human Resources 71
Specialists, Labor Relations 129
Specialists, Market Research Analysts 85
Specialists, Occupational Health and Safety 71
Specialists, Public Relations 89
Specialists, Skincare 61
Specialists, Training 71
Statisticians 84
Superintendents, Postmasters and Mail 101
Supervisors, Aircraft Cargo Handling 86
Surfacing 136
Surgeons 57
Surveyors 67

T

Tailors 75
Teachers, Adult Basic Education and Literacy 107
Teachers, Elementary School 107
Teachers, Kindergarten 107
Teachers, Special Education 108
Tech, Environmental Engineering 132
Tech, Environmental Science and Protection 49
Tech, Industrial Engineering 131
Tech, Medical Records and Health Info 49
Technicians, Agricultural and Food Science 90
Technicians, Avionics 86
Technicians, Biological 49
Technicians, Civil Engineering 82
Technicians, Forensic Science 87
Technicians, Forest Conservation 101
Technicians, Geo and Petroleum 131
Technicians, Ophthalmic Laboratory 60
Technicians, Ophthalmic Medical 60
Technicians, Sound Engineering 117
Technicians, Wind Turbine Service 127
Technologists, Cardiovascular 48
Technologists, Food Scientists and 90
Technologists, Magnetic Resonance Imaging 55
Technologists, Nuclear Medicine 55
Technologists, Radiologic 48
Technologists, Surgical 56
Technologists, Veterinary 50
Telemarketers 119
Therapists, Marriage and Family 61
Therapists, Massage 58
Therapists, Occupational 59

INDEX

Therapists, Physical 59
Therapists, Radiation 52
Therapists, Recreational 58
Therapists, Respiratory 48
Tractor-Trailer, Heavy and 137
Trades, Supervisors / Managers of Construction 131
Trainers, Athletic 59
Translators, Interpreters and 83
Truck, Bus and 135
Typists, Word Processors and 119

U

Undertakers, Morticians and 93

V

Vessels, Captains and Pilots of Water 70
Veterinarians 50

W

Welders 134
Workers, and School Social 103
Workers, Animal Control 102
Workers, Community Health 61
Workers, Grounds Maintenance 132
Workers, Healthcare Social 48, 103
Workers, Highway Maintenance 136
Workers, Manager of Retail Sales 80
Workers, Mental Health Substance Abuse Social 103
Workers, Pest Control 130
Workers, Sheet Metal 134
Workers, Supervisors Fire Fighting 110
Writers, Technical 83

Made in the USA
Monee, IL
14 February 2022